John 1.

THE COMPLETE IDIOT'S GUIDE® TO

Bible Study
for Teens

As were out together dancing cheek to cheek

Pastor William R. Grimbol

ALPHA
A Pearson Education Company

This book is dedicated to my son, Justin Trevor Rannie Grimbol, who is my mentor on all matters of faith and youth.

Copyright © 2002 by William R. Grimbol

International Standard Book Number: 0-02-864274-0
Library of Congress Catalog Card Number: 2001097248

04 03 02   8 7 6 5 4 3 2 1

Interpretation of the printing code: The rightmost number of the first series of numbers is the year of the book's printing; the rightmost number of the second series of numbers is the number of the book's printing. For example, a printing code of 02-1 shows that the first printing occurred in 2002.

Printed in the United States of America

Note: This publication contains the opinions and ideas of its author. It is intended to provide helpful and informative material on the subject matter covered. It is sold with the understanding that the author and publisher are not engaged in rendering professional services in the book. If the reader requires personal assistance or advice, a competent professional should be consulted.

The author and publisher specifically disclaim any responsibility for any liability, loss, or risk, personal or otherwise, which is incurred as a consequence, directly or indirectly, of the use and application of any of the contents of this book.

Publisher: Marie Butler-Knight
Product Manager: Phil Kitchel
Managing Editor: Jennifer Chisholm
Senior Acquisitions Editor: Randy Ladenheim-Gil
Development Editor: Nancy D. Warner
Senior Production Editor: Christy Wagner
Copy Editor: Nancy Wagner
Illustrator: Jody Schaffer
Cover Designers: Kurt Owens and Trina Wurst
Book Designer: Trina Wurst
Layout/Proofreading: Angela Calvert, Mary Hunt, Vicki Keller

Contents

Part 1: Bible Basics 101   1

1 What Is the Bible?   1

The Bible as Testimony 2

The Bible as Story 5

The Bible as Myth 6

The Bible as Poetry 7

The Bible and Humanity 8

The Bible as Comedy *8*

The Bible as Tragedy *8*

The Bible as a Fairy Tale 9

The Gospel Truth 10

2 Who Wrote the Bible?   13

J, E, P, and D 14

Priests 15

Prophets 15

Judges and Kings 17

The Four Gospel Writers (Editors) 17

Matthew *18*

Mark *18*

Luke *19*

John *19*

Paul 20

Ghostwriters 21

Part 2: Hebrew Scripture: The People   23

3 The Covenants   25

Creation Is a Covenant 26

Noah and the Flood 27

The Tower of Babel 28

The Covenant with Abraham 29

The Covenant with Isaac 31

The Covenant with Jacob 32
The Story of Joseph 33

4 The Exodus   35

Moses 36
Let My People Go! 38
Exit Stage Right 40
The First Outward-Bound Program 41
The Ten Commandments Are Not
    Multiple Choice 42
A Lot of Bull 45
Leviticus, Numbers, and Deuteronomy 45
Exodus as Spiritual Paradigm 47

5 The Judges   49

Joshua 50
The Tribal Confederacy 52
Battling Baal 53
12 for 410 54
Uncle Samuel 55

Part 3: Hebrew Scripture: The Nation   59

6 The Kings   61

Saul the Sad 62
    Saul's Top and Bottom Ten *63*
David the Divine 64
Solomon the Splendid 66

7 The Prophets of Israel   71

Jeroboam I 72
The House of Omri 73
The Role of the Prophets 74
A Trio of Prophetic Troublers 75
    Elijah the Tishbite *76*
    Elisha the Wonder Full *77*
Amos: The Herdsman from Tekoa 78
Hosea and Gomer 80

8 The Prophets of Judah   83

The Reign of Uzziah 84

Isaiah and the Blistered Lips 85

Micah, the Rural Prophet 88

Jeremiah and the Tattooed Heart 89

Ezekiel the Priest 91

9 The Poets   95

The Psalter 96

The Wisdom Literature 98

Ecclesiastes *99*

Proverbs *100*

Job *101*

The Song of Solomon 103

Part 4: Christian Scripture:
**   Jesus' Beginnings   105**

10 In the Beginning—the Sequel   107

Jesus' Life 108

Prophesy Fulfilled 108

O Come, O Come, Immanuel (Isaiah 7:10–17) *109*

The Messianic King (Isaiah 9:1–7) *109*

The Servant Songs (Isaiah 42:1–4, 49:1–6,
*   50:4–9, 52:13–53:12)* *110*

The Good Shepherd (Ezekiel 34:1–31) *110*

An Answer for Job (Job 38:1–41:34) *111*

Something New Under the Sun (Ecclesiastes 1:1–18) 111

The Traditional Christmas Story (Luke 2:1–20) 112

Herod and the Astrologers (Matthew 2:1–12) 115

The Wonder Years 116

Rebel with a Cause 118

11 Jesus and the Disciples   119

Who Were the Twelve? 120

Why These Guys? 121

Why Were They Such Lousy Friends? *123*

Where Were the Women? *123*

The Duties of a Disciple 124
A Ministry of Mercy 126
The Courage of the First Disciples 127

Part 5: Christian Scripture: Jesus' Ministry 129

12 Jesus the Preacher: The Sermon on the Mount   131

The Beatitudes = the Being Attitudes
(Matthew 5:1–11) 132
Grace and the Law 135
Handling Hard Emotions 137
Vows and Commitments (Matthew 5:31–37) 137
Faithful and Fruitful 138
Money Matters (Matthew 6:19–24) 139
Judgementalness (Matthew 7:1–6) 140
Worry Warts (Matthew 6:25–34) 141

13 Jesus as Teacher: The Parables   143

What Is a Parable? 144
Just a Pinch Is Plenty 145
It's Yeasting! 145
The Pricey Pearl 146
Does Anyone Have Any Grey Poupon? 147
It's the Soil, Stupid! 148
Lost and Found 149
The Lost Sheep (Luke 15:1–7) 150
The Lost Coin (Luke 15:8–10) 150
The Lost Son (Luke 15:11–32) 150
The Upside of Down 151
The Loser Banquet (Luke 14:15–24) 152
The Good Samaritan (Luke 10:25–37) 152
The Parable of Wages (Matthew 20:1–16) 154
Plenty of Parables 155

14 Jesus as Healer: The Miracles   157

Can Miracles Really Happen? 158
Miracles vs. Fear 159
  The Paralyzed Man (Mark 2:1–12) 160
  The Healing at the Pool (John 5:1–18) 161
  The Roman Officer's Servant (Luke 7:1–10) 162
Miracles vs. Demons 163
  A Boy and His Demon (Matthew 17:14–21) 163
  My Name Is Legion (Mark 5:1–20) 164
Miracles vs. Nature 165
  Jesus Calms a Storm (Matthew 8:23–27) 166
  Jesus Feeds Five Thousand (John 6:1–15) 167
  Jesus Walks on Water (John 6:16–21) 167
A Review of Miracles in Christian Scripture 168
Healings and Miracles—a Summary 172

15 Jesus as Prophet: Passion Week   173

His Message 174
The Triumphant Entry to Jerusalem
  (Luke 19:28–44) 175
Jesus Clears the Temple (Mark 11:15–19) 177
Jesus' Authority Is Challenged (Mark 11:27–33) 178
  *Jesus Faces More Stiff Questioning by the
    Pharisees (Mark 12:13–34)* 179
  *Jesus Warns Against the Religious Establishment
    (Mark 12:38–40)* 179
  The Olivet Discourse (Mark 13) 179
The Last Supper (Mark 14:17–31) 180
  The Upper Room (John 13–17) 181
  The Garden of Gethsemane (Mark 14:32–42) 181
  Jesus Betrayed and Arrested (Mark 14:43–52) 181
The Trial 182
The Crucifixion (Mark 15:20–41) 182

Part 6: Christian Scripture: Jesus as the Christ   185

16 Opening Paul's Mail   187

Paul—Born Again? 188

Paul's Ministry 189

Paul's Gospel 190

The Grace of God 190

The Law 191

Fools for Christ 191

Christ Who Lives in Me 192

The Life in the Spirit 192

Paul and the Church 193

Paul's Top Ten 196

17 The Disciples Act Up and Out (Acts)   197

The Book of Acts 198

Pentecost (Acts 2:1–13) 198

Peter—Part One (Acts 1–5) 200

Stephen (Acts 6–7) 200

Philip (Acts 6:1–7, 8:5–40, 21:8–10) 202

Peter—Part Two (Acts 9–12) 203

Paul (Acts 13:1–28:31) 203

The Cast and Crew 204

The Gospel of Acts 205

18 The First New Age Movement (The Book of Revelation)   207

Will the Real John Please Stand Up? 208

Apocalyptic Literature 209

Rome 210

Rome = the Beast 211

Rome = Babylon 212
What Was Happening in the Church? 214
The Seven Visions 214
The New Age 215
Summary of the Main Points of Revelation 216

Introduction

The Bible. What a huge topic for such a small book. Can I do it justice? Probably not. Does that make my writing and your reading pointless? Not at all. It simply means that this book must be viewed as only a beginning. At best it will be a catalyst for further study. At the very least, it will give you enough background information so as not to feel stupid on the subject.

My first encounter with the Bible came at the home of my grandmother. She kept an enormous Bible on an end table in the living room. It was easily six inches thick. The cover was hardened leather. The lettering on the front was bold and gold. The pages were laced with curlicues. It was difficult to lift, and simply opening it took effort.

The pages were in mint condition. Clean. Shiny. Often sticking together. I do not recall ever seeing a member of my family using that Bible—I mean using it to read. On hot humid summer nights, this Bible did serve as a doorstop to let in the breezes off Lake Michigan.

I thought of that Bible as a treasure chest. I was secretly eager to sift my fingers through the gems and pearls and gold inside. I am not sure why or how, but I had come to believe that you needed a treasure map in order to gain entrance. Having no such map, I did not feel entitled to look inside.

There was another Bible in my grandmother's home. This one was small and red and sat next to her bed. It was worn and smudged and dog-eared. This Bible was filled with little notes Grandma had written to herself. When I occasionally slept over, I would hear Grandma sigh or say "Yes" as she read. She would often clutch that book to her chest, as if it were a child, as if she hoped to squeeze out the very last drop of "something." I knew that Grandma loved that book. She cherished it.

On one such sleepover, I asked her to read me something, hoping I might be ready to receive the treasure map. She read me a story about a guy named Jonah and a great big whale. I found the story silly, and I could not imagine what the big deal was. I didn't know anyone named Jonah. I had never seen a whale. I found my comic books far more exciting and the characters more believable. My disappointment was as massive as that living room Bible.

As a teenager my feelings about the Bible went from mysterious to just plain confused. Everybody seemed to have an opinion about the Bible, but I suspected nobody had really read it. Some of my more religious friends would randomly spout Bible verses, but it never seemed to affect or alter their behavior, and it reminded me of childhood nursery rhymes. I found the adults who claimed to know the Bible inside out stiff, strict, and judgmental. Though almost everybody claimed the Bible to be special, important, even holy, nobody seemed able to explain why.

By the time I was in high school I had come to the following conclusions about the Bible:

- The Bible was seldom read.
- Even with not having read it, most adults thought they knew what the Bible had to say.
- Most teenagers felt the Bible was for old people.
- The Bible had something to do with faith and God.
- The Bible had little to do with life.
- Bible had nothing to do with *my* life.
- In Sunday School I learned that the God of the Hebrew Scriptures was often angry, mean, and prone to violence.
- In Confirmation I learned that the God of the Christian Scriptures had somehow become much nicer—even friendly.

Other than that, I didn't much care what the Bible had to say. I no longer saw it as a jewel-jammed treasure chest. To my mind it was just another old trunk in the attic—not of much use, gathering dust, fun to rummage through on a rainy day when there was nothing else to do.

But I remained haunted by those images of my grandmother reading and sighing, her whispered "Yes," how she squeezed her Bible to her chest. What was it that Grandma had found in the pages of that book? My grandmother was no dummy. She was bright. She was wise. She was as good a person as I knew. To this day I believe that it was those images of Grandma, a seed of a kind, that blossomed as a desire in me to explore the Bible.

Each of us has a story. The story of our relationship to the Bible. A story that has shaped and formed our attitude about the Bible. A story that sprouted like a seed into a wish, a need, a desire to know more.

Before you read the chapters of this book, ask yourself why you picked it up. Did someone purchase it for you? Who? Why? Before you begin, know what it is that brought you to reading these pages. Trust me. Knowing your motivation will determine much of what you receive from this little book.

This book is aimed at you, the teenager. I refuse to talk down to you. I will not treat you as a child. I also will not deal with you as a sophisticated adult. I like adolescents. I love writing for adolescents. It is your nature to doubt, question, and struggle with what you hear and read. That makes for an exciting dialogue between author and reader. It also demands brutally honest writing. I promise you that.

The Bible is often referred to as the Word of God. I believe that. I also happen to believe that the Creation is an expression of the Word. Life is soaked in it. We are well-dipped. One thing is for sure: The Bible does contain a heck of a lot of words. The holiness of those words. The idea that they are directly inspired by God. That is a matter of faith. Only your heart can know.

Some Things to Help Out Along the Way

On almost every page of this book you will find an information box. These boxes are there to highlight important ideas. I have chosen to identify these boxes with word-related themes. These information boxes will be labeled as follows:

In a Word or Two

In a Word or Two boxes contain important quotes from important thinkers.

A Bad Word

A Bad Word boxes are warnings about how *not* to read the Bible or what the Bible does *not* say.

Password

Definitions of vital words or concepts can be found in Password boxes.

Spread the Good Word

These boxes give you direct quotations from the Bible.

The Good Word

These boxes contain helpful tips that will deepen your understanding of the Bible.

I have promised you honest writing. I need you to be an honest, reader. I need your heart and mind to be present in the reading. I need you to be free to approach this book and the Bible itself, on your terms. No prejudices. No preconceived notions. As best you can, with no religious bias. Grant yourself the chance to engage me honestly and openly in a dialogue on this magnificent book—the Bible. I will leave the label Holy Bible up to you and your faith.

Acknowledgments

I wish to thank Randy Ladenheim-Gil for her patient perseverance, as well as her kindness in bringing this book to fruition. I am also indebted to Christy Wagner, the senior production editor, Nancy Warner, the development editor, and Nancy Wagner, the copy editor. This author is immensely appreciative of the editing process and grateful for the competence of this trio. I also wish to say thanks to Alpha Books and to Marie Butler-Knight, for giving me the chance to write and the creative context in which to share my ideas and beliefs with youth.

Note on the Scripture Passages

The scripture passages given throughout the book are from the *Life Application Study Bible, New Living Translation* (Tundale House Publishers, Inc.).

Trademarks

All terms mentioned in this book that are known to be or are suspected of being trademarks or service marks have been appropriately capitalized. Alpha Books and Pearson Education, Inc., cannot attest to the accuracy of this information. Use of a term in this book should not be regarded as affecting the validity of any trademark or service mark.

Bible Basics 101

No matter what I write about the Bible or how I say it, this book will be controversial. The Bible is always a hot potato. There will be raised eyebrows, nods of approval, and scowls of scorn. There will be things I miss. Important stories will be omitted. Key players will not be named. To cover everything would require a book as long as the Bible itself. I simply wish to provide a reasonable overview of the biblical material.

Part 1 seeks to answer the big questions about the Bible—who wrote it? what is it about? when was it written? where?—and the more complex issues of why it was written and how. It will also share with you my perspective on approaching the Bible. Each person sees the Bible through a different lens. Each of us will have a different take on the concept—the Word of God.

Chapter

What Is the Bible?

In This Chapter

- The Bible as a testimony of faith
- The Bible contains ample historical fact
- The Bible is often written as myth
- The Bible contains magnificent poetry
- The Bible functions as comedy, tragedy, and even fairy tale
- The Bible claims to be the gospel truth and is claimed by many to be the same

For me, the Bible is a grand patchwork quilt made up of stories, myths, poetry, history, facts, faith-fiction, and fairy tale. What I believe holds all these patches together, the sacred thread, is the love of God. The patches themselves are at times frayed, soiled, stained, or torn by the humanity of their authors. The thread, however, remains strong, the stitching true, the unseen knots tight. Piece by piece it may seem no more than rags. As a whole, it is a magnificent thing.

You can't read the Bible like a history book, nor can you use it like a blueprint. The Bible contains too much mystery for that—too much faith.

The writers of Scripture felt compelled to share their faith. They wanted us to know about their God and to understand their relationship with God, and they needed us to know why their God was vital to their lives. There is hardly a sentence of Scripture that is not coated with faith.

As you read this chapter, you will gain insight into how the Bible came into being, its evolution. You will come to understand the many styles of Scripture. This chapter seeks to trace the movement of the Spirit and to enable you to discern the handwriting of God. The Bible did not come out of nowhere. It was not sent from Heaven by fax. It came from folks right here on earth. It is the story of many stories and storytellers.

The Bible as Testimony

Testimony, when given at a trial as evidence is a declaration of how a person sees something. It is a statement of conviction. If found to be false, it is a reason for conviction. If found to be true, it is because the testimony was believed. In the case of the Bible, the testimony is given as evidence of the presence of God. What is often on trial is the faith in that presence.

I will use Hebrew Scripture when speaking of what is traditionally called the Old Testament. "Old" implies past or outdated. Hebrew Scripture speaks more accurately to the fact that the Jewish faith is alive and well. I will also refer to the New Testament as Christian Scripture.

In a Word or Two

[Jesus], a man who was completely innocent, offered himself as a sacrifice for the good of others, including his enemies, and became the ransom of the world. It was a perfect act.

—Mohandas K. Gandhi, *Non-Violence in Peace and War* (1948)

The Hebrew Scriptures (the Old Testament of the Bible) tell of the extraordinary spiritual odyssey of the Jewish people. It is a record of their faith and of their lives. It is a political, social, and economic document. It is also deeply religious and declares that the Jewish people were chosen to be God's own people. It gives evidence of God's guidance throughout their history and expresses the conviction that Israel is a promised and holy land.

The Hebrew Scripture reveals an intimate relationship between God and his people. God is actively involved in every facet of Hebrew life: God is sought for counsel in times of sorrow; he must listen to endless complaints; he is the target of anger and doubt; and he is expected to heap on blessings for good behavior. God is their God: He is to be on their side in war; he must provide food in times of famine; he is their personal protector; he is understood as the champion of his people.

The Hebrew Scripture is one wild ride. There are the days of despair, when the Hebrew people were forced into slavery, and days of power, during the reign of David and the days of Solomon's opulence and splendor. The Scripture is jammed with stories of the great faith of the Jewish people, as well as tales of faithlessness. The biblical prophets are either scolding their people for their disobedience or promising them the good fruits of obedience. We read poetry of great gentleness and beauty and history of unparalleled savagery. Ecclesiastes wails that all is vanity. God shouts that all is good.

In a Word or Two

As soon as God decided to take a hand in history, he had to start somewhere. What he elected to start with was Israel. This election has been a constant source of dismay, delight, and embarrassment to them both ever since. The account of the first few millennia of their stormy affair is contained in the Old Testament.

—Frederick Buechner, *Wishful Thinking*

The Christian Scriptures (the New Testament of the Bible) focus on Jesus the man. We read of his ministry to the poor and the outcast. Jesus' message was simply that the first will be last, and the last first. He also stated that the rich will be sent away empty, and the poor will know great abundance. The value system of Jesus was a complete transformation of that of the world. We are told of miraculous healings and events: Jesus walks on water; Jesus feeds 5,000 with just a few fish and loaves of bread; Jesus raises Lazarus from the dead. Testimony is abundant that this is no ordinary man.

Jesus is described as a man of pure goodness. He is pictured as a man whose heart bleeds with compassion for all those in need—physical, emotional, or spiritual. He is thought to be the event of *grace* itself. His disciples are simple working men who adore him and yet miserably fail him. When Jesus is tragically crucified, his band of followers disperse in despair.

Jesus is *resurrected*. His tomb is left empty. He appears to his dazzled and bewildered disciples. His resurrection forms the central piece of evidence that he is the long-sought *Messiah*. The early church is built upon a foundation of faith in his divinity.

Password

Grace is the belief that God's love is without conditions, it is absolute and available to all. **Messiah,** in Hebrew, means "the one anointed by God," just as a king might be anointed. In Greek, the word means "Christ." **Resurrection** is a belief that life is eternal. Eternal life is not endless life or time. It is life totally transformed. It is the absence of time. It is like the experience of losing track of time.

In both the Hebrew and Christian Scriptures, the testimony given is to prove the active presence of God in the lives of those who believe.

The Bible as Story

You are at a family reunion. The picnic supper is served. The table chatter begins. You wince as the old stories begin to be tossed back and forth around the table. Your uncles still laugh at the same points. Your aunts once again lovingly point out the glaring inaccuracies of the tale. Grandma agrees. Grandpa says the story is 100 percent true. The little cousins ask to hear more. You act bored and annoyed but wonder when your turn will come to tell one of the family stories. You listen. The stories always change, just a bit, and yet remain the same. Your heart tells you that these are special stories, sacred stories.

Stories. Are they fact or fiction? They are both. All good stories are composed of real historical events. They are also coated in layer upon layer of memory, love, want, need, and faith. Each story is altered not only by time but also by the human condition as well. If the family needs to laugh, the story becomes funnier. If the family needs to be inspired, the tale is woven with courage. If the family feels the need to be warned, the tone of the story becomes more ominous.

In a Word or Two

Fiction is like a spider's web, attached ever so slightly perhaps, but still attached to life at all four corners.

—Virginia Woolf, *A Room of One's Own*

The Bible is full of such stories. These stories of family, of the human family, of the faith family. These stories were first spoken and passed on orally. Are they true? Are they fiction? Would you call the stories of your family fiction? I call the stories of my family the gospel truth—a truth only understood by the listening heart.

The Bible as Myth

In the West we use the word *myth* to mean "falsehood." In the East, where the Bible was written, a myth is a story that is always true. Myths try to reveal the mind of God. Myths try to capture the human heart, to speak directly to the soul. Myths tell us about ourselves.

I think of myths as being dreamlike. A dream may be shaped and formed from the day's events, yet it is not the day. A dream often reveals the truth of the day, whether it was filled with worry or fear or joy.

I think of the Creation story as such a myth. It does not read like history. There certainly was no reporter there recording the facts. No, this story is telling me something deeper, something that goes to my very core. I believe it is telling me that God is in charge; that life is good; that God loves every created thing—even the slithering snake. The Creation story is a dream come true. It is a tale that is truer than true—and too good not to be true.

I know it will be hard for many readers to hear the Creation story labeled a myth. For many folks, the Creation story must be taken as literal truth. The Creation happened exactly as it is written. That may be true. I mean that. Who am I to say that it could not possibly have happened that way? Why would I want to tell someone that his belief is wrong? In matters of faith, all we can legitimately share is what we believe—our version.

For me, as a literal truth, the story makes little sense and even less of an impact. As a myth, it makes uncommon sense. A myth does not strive to prove something as fact or declare it as certainty. A myth tries to move us. To shake us up. To shake our foundations. A myth seeks to jar loose the faith that is stuck deep inside us.

For example, have you ever fallen in love? If so, imagine being asked to write a story to prove your love. What evidence would you offer? What testimony would you give? How would you create a story to express the depth of your love? Whatever you write would be mostly myth. Try it for yourself.

A Bad Word

Beware of the person who claims to have all the answers. Beware of the person who believes his answer is the only answer. Beware of the person who believes his or her answer to be superior. These folks seldom inspire faith. More often than not, they kill it. For every person they turn on, they turn five off.

The Bible as Poetry

Have you ever written a poem? It is a journey. The destination is in sight but unknown. Words, like stops along the way, are chosen with great care. The writing is slow. It may be painful. Poetry is how we seek to share our wonder or amazement.

If I said that the waves beat against the shore like a thousand mad fists, you would not run down to the beach to look for a bunch of human hands. You would know that I was speaking in poetic imagery, that I was using a metaphor. You would also know that the waves were big. You would know exactly what I wanted you to know—the condition of the sea was angry.

The use of metaphors is common in the Bible. Jesus is called the Bread of Life, Living Water, the Great Shepherd, and a Lamb. Metaphors are symbols. The symbol reveals the essence, the heart and soul. Obviously, these metaphors cannot be taken literally.

The Bible is also filled with poetry—the Psalms, Ecclesiastes, and the Gospel of Luke. Poetry is an essential tool in the composition of Scripture. Poetry strives to reveal the essence of an event, emotion, or experience. The biblical poets had both a passion for words and their beliefs.

Biblical poetry, like all poetry, seeks to capture in words what cannot be captured in words. I know—that sounds crazy. It is crazy. It would also be crazy not to attempt to express what we believe. The biblical poets, like all poets, do their best to paint the color of the wind. I have come to believe that poetry is the language of truth.

In a Word

True poetry, the best of it, is but the ashes of a burnt-out passion.

—Oliver Wendell Holmes Sr., *Over the Teacups* (1891)

The Bible and Humanity

Being a human being is often comical, yet it can also be quite tragic. Embracing this reality is critical to maturity. Without the tragedy or the comedy, there would be no growth and little faith.

The Bible as Comedy

The Bible is at times a comedy. Our reaction to reading it is often "You have got to be kidding!" Abraham and Sarah are told by an angel that they will have a child when they are both in their 90s. The child's name is Isaac, which in Hebrew means "laughter." God chooses Moses, a murderer, to lead his people. God chooses the Jews, who someone said are like everyone else but more so. Jesus chooses 12 disciples who, by background and nature, can hardly agree on a thing.

Often times the Bible reads like a joke. We humans frequently are the punch line. Only faith enables us to get the joke.

The Bible as Tragedy

The Bible is clearly loaded with tragedy. What happens to people of faith is often brutal and wicked. Faith does not erase evil. Faith is forced to coexist with evil. The Bible is often very bad news before it becomes good news.

Before the Jews find the Promised Land, they are held for years as slaves in Egypt. Their wandering in the wilderness is a long and spiritual struggle. Their faith is not only severely tested, but at times lost altogether. They wind up worshipping a golden bull and plotting to overthrow Moses, who many have come to believe has gotten them hopelessly lost.

The story of Jesus is pure tragedy. His ministry of help, hope, and healing results only in rousing the wrath of many. The majority of folks do not see him as a Messiah, but as a problematic trouble-maker. His crucifixion is, in some respects, inexplicable and yet in other ways, totally predictable. The truth is seldom welcomed by society. Those who champion the poor and outcast often pay a huge price.

The Bible as a Fairy Tale

The Bible as a fairy tale? This is bound to ruffle some feathers. But why? What is a fairy tale? It is make-believe. It is a story told to make us believe. It is a story that tells a truth—at times a gospel truth.

Once upon a time …. The beginning of a fairy tale sets the story in eternity. It is a story with a message for all people for all time.

The traditional story of the birth of Jesus, found in the Gospel of Luke 2:1–20, is written like a fairy tale: It is set in the common-place; it is rooted in fact and objective history; there was a Mary and Joseph; there was a birth that probably did take place in a stable.

Yet there are also all the wonderful trappings of a fairy tale: Beth-lehem the enchanted village lit by the light of an extraordinary star; the heralding of angels; the singing shepherds; the travelling wise men from the East; the symbolic gifts of gold, frankincense, and myrrh; the illuminated stable which draws the world in. Mary and Joseph who both know that this is no ordinary birth. The whole story is composed like a fairy tale—to make us believe.

Consider *The Wizard of Oz*. Is it just a fairy tale? Why was it writ-ten? I believe it was written to reveal many truths: that life can be a whirlwind. That we at times lose track of our hearts, minds, and courage and must risk the adventure of hunting to find them. That

we must face our witches. That wizards can only give back to us
what we already possess. That we must come full circle to the wisdom that there is no place like home.

The Gospel Truth

The gospel truth. Have you heard or used that phrase? It speaks of
a truth that is truer than true. It is when we mean something from
the bottom of our hearts. It is when we passionately want our words
to be trusted. Speaking the gospel truth is when we are asking the
listener to believe us. We are in effect saying, "Please have faith in
what I am saying. Please have faith in me." The entire Bible can be
thought of as an expression of the gospel truth.

The Least You Need to Know

- The Bible is a vast collection of stories which contain ample
  historical fact and events but are encased in the testimonial
  language of faith.
- Many Bible stories are written as myth or poetry.
- Bible stories are frequently comic or tragic. Some are written
  in the spirit of fairy tales—to make us believe.
- The Bible seeks to express a gospel truth—a truth which cannot be proved, yet is still believed.

Chapter 2

Who Wrote the Bible?

In This Chapter

- The Bible was first transmitted orally
- The first five books of the Bible and four sources of the Pentateuch
- The Hebrew Scriptures were also written by priests, prophets, judges, and kings
- The four Gospel writers of Christian Scripture are Matthew, Mark, Luke, and John
- Paul's letters to the early church are personal and pastoral
- The Bible had a great many ghostwriters

The Bible is shaped and formed from stories—stories which were first transmitted orally. Many were probably first told around the fire under a blanket of stars. They were spread from home to village to nation. If it was a good story, a really good story, it spread like wildfire. However, unlike a piece of gossip, which also spreads rapidly, a good story lays down deep roots. A good story lasts. The good stories of the Bible appear to be eternal.

The Bible owes a huge debt to these storytellers. The oral tradition is the passing on of stories, history, laws, prayers, and poetry from one generation to the next.

As you read this chapter, you will come to know a good deal more about the Bible's many authors. You will learn about the four great sources of Hebrew Scripture—J, E, P, and D—and the four gospel writers of Christian Scripture—Matthew, Mark, Luke, and John. You will examine the role of prophets, priests, judges, and kings in shaping Hebrew Scripture. You will explore the unique and powerful position of Paul in forming the early church and authoring over half the books of Christian Scripture. Most important, you will come to see how the many voices of Scripture become a chorus, all giving praise and thanksgiving to God.

J, E, P, and D

No, this is not a New Age rock group. J, E, P, and D are considered the primary sources for the Pentateuch, or the first five books of the Bible. These five books are also known collectively as the Torah, a work of Jewish law composed of Genesis, Exodus, Leviticus, Numbers, and Deuteronomy.

The writers who put together these sources made good use of oral material, as well as some in written form. The material used was ancient.

- "J" was a writer who gets his name from the consistent use of Yahweh (Jehovah) as the name for God (composed during the reigns of kings David and Solomon, 1000–922 B.C.).

- "E" used the name "Elohim"—divine being (composed during the eighth century A.D.).

- "P" is a source that was primarily interested in the role and responsibilities of the priests (composed during the time of the exile, 577–539 B.C.).

- "D" is for Deuteronomy and is the major source of that book (composed around 650 B.C.).

Priests

The Hebrew Scripture had many authors. Authorship was reserved for men of education and those who played a significant role in society and the life of the Temple.

The priesthood in biblical thought symbolized God's union with Israel. Israel was meant to be a kingdom of priests. Since God is holy, Israel must be a holy nation. The word *priest* occurs more than 700 times in Hebrew scriptures.

There were three levels of priests:

- At the top was the *high priest*. The high priesthood was a position of great power and splendor. The high priest possessed the same dignity as a king. Joshua was a high priest. When Israel was ruled by priests, this was called a heirocracy.

- The second level was the *ordinary priest*. These men were cultic specialists. There were 24 priestly families who took turns caring for the Temple. Priests were responsible for the sacred vessels of the sanctuary and the sacrificial duties of the altar. The priests were highly respected in the community, helped to administer justice, and were sought for medical advice. A priest was required to have no physical defects (for example, leprosy).

- The third level was the *Levites*. They were to assist the priests and serve the congregation. The Levites cleaned and cared for the sacred vessels, prepared the cereal offerings, and were the sanctuary custodians.

Prophets

Prophets believed that they were instruments of God's will, sent by God to deliver a message. Their authority came directly from God. Their task was to communicate God's message for now and to call on God's people to respond today. Prophets were not concerned with predicting the future; they were urgently concerned with the present.

There were three primary classifications of prophets:

- **Ecstatic prophets.** Ecstatic prophesy meant that an individual was overwhelmed not only by emotion, but also by the presence of God. They believed God had taken control of their being. There were roving bands of ecstatic prophets called schools who lived in communities under the leadership of a chief prophet.

- **Cultic prophets.** These were the prophets closely associated with the great sanctuaries of Israel. They were regarded as experts in prayer and were called upon to bring the petitions of the people to God. They were also entrusted with bringing God's answer to the people.

- **Political prophets.** Prophesy is intimately associated with politics. These were the prophets who often championed a holy war. The great prophets, however, often were not servants of nationalism but asserted that God would punish Israel for disobedience.

A Bad Word

Many today think of prophesy as fortune-telling. Wrong! Prophets were messengers, men who spoke for God. Prophesy was all about faith, not making money.

It was believed at this time that there were three acceptable ways to know the will of God: dreams, the sacred dice of the Temple, and prophesy.

The Hebrew Scriptures contain the writing of a great many prophets, notably Amos, Hosea, Isaiah, Micah, Jeremiah, Ezekiel, Elijah, and Elisha. To be honest, we can trace prophecy back to Moses, as well as to the ministry of Jesus and the early church. The role of prophecy was to witness to God's dynamic participation in history. In their own way, Martin Luther King and Malcolm X were contemporary prophets.

Judges and Kings

After the death of Joshua, the high priest, the Israelite confederacy came to be ruled by judges. The confederacy was a loose collection of tribes. These judges were chosen because ...

- They had shown themselves to be effective military leaders.
- They possessed great charisma.
- They were thought to be wise.
- They were believed to be faithful.

Samuel would become the greatest and most revered of these judges. Israel moved from confederacy to nationhood with the emergence of a monarchy. Saul was Israel's first king. David would bring Israel to the full status of nationhood. Solomon transformed Israel into a nation of splendor. These were the three great kings of Hebrew Scripture.

David is believed to have written over 70 of the Psalms. Solomon is credited with a few Psalms, most of the Proverbs, and Ecclesiastes. It is important to note that the political leaders of Israel were also significant spiritual guides. The fact that kings wrote Scripture is essential to any real understanding of the Bible.

The Four Gospel Writers (Editors)

The Christian Scripture is dominated by four gospels (meaning "good news"). The Gospels are four versions of the same story, four unique perspectives. Matthew, Mark, Luke, and John were the editors of the Gospels. Editors seek to assemble material in such a way as to take a stand or to make a particular point. These four men each offer a different vantage point to the ministry and message of Jesus.

Matthew

Matthew was dependent on Mark in composing his gospel. He writes an orderly, but not chronological, account of the life of Jesus. Matthew must have lived in a Greek-speaking community because his gospel was originally written in Greek. Matthew is primarily concerned with communicating the gospel to Jewish people. He records nine events that are not found in the other gospels:

- The dream of Joseph (1:20–24)
- The visit of the astrologers (2:1–12)
- The escape to Egypt (2:13–15)
- The slaughter of the children (2:16–18)
- The death of Judas (27:3–10)
- The dream of Pilate's wife (27:19)
- The resurrections of others (27:52)
- The bribery of the guards (28:11–15)
- The emphasis on baptism in the great commissioning (28:19–20)

Each of these nine special events would have helped Matthew make his case to the Jews. For example, since dreams were believed by the Jews to be a medium of God's will, the dreams mentioned here would have taken on added significance. Matthew's goal was to provide clear and compelling evidence that Jesus was the Messiah.

Mark

This gospel was written just before the fall of Jerusalem to the Roman army in 70 A.D. It is thought to have been written by John Mark, who accompanied Paul on his first missionary journey (Acts 13:13).

Mark's gospel became the core of Matthew's and Luke's versions. All but 31 verses of Mark are quoted in these gospels. This trio—Matthew, Mark, and Luke—is known as the Synoptic Gospels, which means that all three contain the same synopsis—the Marcan outline.

Mark's gospel addresses the role of Jesus in the life of the church. Jesus was to be the subject of preaching, the authority for teaching, and the mediator of worship. In Mark the distinguishing feature of Jesus is that of a *servant*. I use "servant" here, not as in butler or waitress, but as one willing to spiritually serve others. When we serve others, we serve God.

Luke

Luke was a doctor, a Gentile (someone who is not Jewish), and a Greek. He is thought to have been a close friend to Paul. He is also assumed to be the author of Acts. The Gospel of Luke is a comprehensive and beautifully written gospel. Luke is focused on the Gentile. Luke also places a special emphasis on ...

- The role of prayer.
- The important and positive role of women.
- The significant, spiritual role of angels.
- The power of the Holy Spirit.

In this gospel Jesus becomes the champion of the poor and the outcast. Jesus rejects no one. Jesus embraces everyone with grace, and his love and forgiveness are made available to all.

John

The Gospel of John is attributed to John the Apostle. Because the writing appears to have been done in 90 to 100 A.D., however, it is more likely that the author was a disciple of the disciple.

This gospel is quite different from the other three. There is no mention of the famous birth story, Jesus' childhood, the temptation, or the appointment of the disciples. It is written from a unique spiritual perspective.

Of Jesus' eight miracles recorded in the Gospels, six of them are found only in the Gospel of John:

- Turning water into wine (2:1–11)
- Healing the official's son (4:46–54)

- Healing the lame man at the pool of Bethesda (5:1–9)
- Feeding the 5,000 (6:1–14)
- Walking on water (6:15–21)
- Restoring sight to the blind man (9:1–41)
- Raising Lazarus from the dead (11:1–44)
- Showing his disciples how to make an amazing catch of fish (21:1–14)

It is the Gospel of John that most boldly declares that Jesus is the Son of God. This is not just a great moral teacher, not just a very good man, but this is a man who is divine.

Paul

Paul was first a Pharisee, which was a Jewish religious group that zealously followed the laws of the Hebrew scripture. He was also a persecutor of the followers of Jesus and believed Jesus to be yet another false Messiah.

It is claimed that Paul was converted to Christianity as the result of a direct encounter with the risen Christ. This conversion was crucial to the shaping of the early church and is acknowledged three times in the Book of Acts (9:3–19, 22:6–16, and 26:9–23).

Paul's letters account for 14 of the 27 books of Christian Scripture. His ministry and message not only shaped the early church, but his missionary journeys were also largely responsible for the building and maintaining of several churches.

Paul's letters offer ...

- Responses to questions on doctrinal teachings.
- Inspiration on moral and ethical conduct.
- Instruction on how to lead an exemplary Christian life.
- Personal requests.

These letters were not academic treatises. These were letters. Personal. Pastoral. They are the efforts of a spiritual leader to guide and protect his flock.

Ghostwriters

Have you ever tried to mimic a writer? To copy his style? To attempt to see the world through his eyes? I recall my early efforts at creative writing. Some months I was playing Hemingway, sometimes Fitzgerald, and when I was really bold, my favorite, Thomas Wolfe.

Ghostwriters are people who write as if they were someone else. Many of the biblical writers did this. As devoted followers of a spiritual leader, they felt able and compelled to speak in his voice. They worked tirelessly to capture the thought and faith of the one they followed. They were not merely students; they were spiritual clones.

Scholars have debated for centuries over authorship of biblical books, and they will continue to do so. However, whether it is a ghostwriter or the actual prophet or disciple, the intention was the same, the message identical. These ghostwriters wrote as clones of the individual they followed.

The Least You Need to Know

- The Bible was shaped through the oral tradition of passing down stories, history, prayer, poetry, custom, and laws.
- J, E, P, and D were the primary sources for the Pentateuch.
- Hebrew Scripture was formed primarily from the writings of priests, prophets, judges, and kings.
- Christian Scripture was formed by the four gospel writers Matthew, Mark, Luke, and John, as well as Paul.
- Each gospel writer, as well as Paul, offered a unique editorial perspective on the subject—Jesus Christ.
- The Bible had a great many ghostwriters.

Part 2

Hebrew Scripture: The People

Hebrew Scripture is the story of the Jewish people. It is a testimony to their faith—and lack of it. It is a chronicle of their struggles to behave as God's chosen race. It is their history. The Hebrew Scripture is not, however, history in the modern sense. It is a faith history.

The writers of Hebrew Scripture had a definite perspective. They believed that God governed their community of faith. Faith history is the documentation of the experiences and remembrances of that faith community. In a very real way, the Hebrew Scripture is a statement of faith. It is the cataloging of beliefs.

The Hebrew Scripture is about the beginnings of everything—the universe, the earth and all of its inhabitants, faith as a whole, and the community of faith in particular. The faith foundation upon which Hebrew Scripture is built is the belief that not one thing came into being without the power and will of God. God is the Creator. God's power is total and visible in all Creation. Hebrew Scripture contends that all of life's deepest questions point to God as the answer.

Chapter 3

The Covenants

In This Chapter

- The Hebrew Scripture is all about relationship
- The core of a strong relationship is a covenant
- The Book of Genesis begins with the covenants made between God and humankind
- The Patriarchal history examines the covenants God made with Abraham, Isaac, and Jacob
- The story of Joseph

As a minister, I conduct weddings. The booklet I use for such services is titled "The Covenant." A wedding is the act of two human beings making a promise to one another to share their lives together. The vows that are spoken are the promises being made; the rings are symbolic of the unending circle of these vows; the announcement of marriage is a public declaration of commitment; the blessing is an acknowledgment that the commitment is rooted in faith and made within the faith community.

The Hebrew Scripture is about the covenants (a commitment grounded in a promise) made between God and the human race. It is the story of this most intimate relationship, a union as close as that of marriage—maybe even closer. The Hebrew Scripture describes the stormy, passionate, and enduring relationship of the Jewish people and their God. It is a familiar story, a story filled with life's ups and downs.

As in all relationships, there are major disputes and more than a few disappointments. There are times of raw joy and deep satisfaction. There are periods of anger. There are times of wondering if it's all worth it. There are also those times when the love is so strong and sure that it is clear one could not live without it. It is the saga of a relationship defined by love and respect and forgiveness. As I said, it is indeed a marriage-like relationship.

As you read this chapter, you will come to see the powerful intimacy between God and the Hebrew people. The great stories of Genesis, the Creation, the Tower of Babel, the Flood, as well as the history of the Patriarchs, Abraham, Isaac, and Jacob each express the dynamic relationship between God and his people. This chapter will give you a genuine appreciation for the centrality of covenant in Hebrew Scripture.

Creation Is a Covenant

The Book of Genesis was written during or shortly after the Jewish exile in Babylon (587–539 B.C.). In exile, the Jewish people were slaves. Thus, it is fair to say that the Creation myth was composed by the Jews while serving as Babylonian slaves. I find it astounding that at the very time they must have felt most abandoned by their God, they would write a story that declares the fullness of their faith. The Creation account was written in such a way as to say to their captors, "You may think you are in power, in charge of our lives, but it is our God alone who is ultimately in control of everything."

The Creation story was a bold and courageous statement of faith. The full story was recorded in Genesis 1:1–2:3. This story of the Creation comes from the priestly, or "P" tradition (refer to Chapter 2, "Who Wrote the Bible?" if you forget the J, P, D, and E references).

The story is told in the tones of a worship service; the language is formal, and the style is rhythmic. We are told that Creation is an expression of God's will. Human beings are not divine, but we are special, blessed with unique powers and responsibilities.

Spread the Good Word

The heavens speak of the Creator's glory and the sky proclaims God's handiwork.

—Psalm 19:2

As you do not know how the spirit comes to the bones in the womb of a woman with child, so you do not know the work of God who makes everything.

—Ecclesiastes 11:5

The second Creation story—yes, there are two—comes from the "J" source. It is the story of the Garden of Eden and is found in Genesis 2:4–3:24. The Garden of Eden is what is commonly referred to as Paradise. It is the idyllic state of the earth, before humankind was capable of any form of pollution—environmental or spiritual.

The second story tells us that human beings have the ability to be who God created us to be. We are capable of obedience. Our disobedience is usually the result of trying to play God. The will of God is for humans to be human.

Noah and the Flood

Covenants are made; covenants are broken. That is the nature of relationships. That is the story of life and the primary theme of Hebrew Scripture.

The story of Noah and the Flood continues to explore God's relationship with humankind. The story is recorded in Genesis 6–9.

These chapters declare that God is not only active in human history but also judges that history. Creation is not left to its own devices. Creation is intended to declare the glory of God.

You most likely know the gist of this famous story ... God is terribly frustrated by the ongoing disobedience of human beings. Human-kind incessantly tries to live as though they have no need for God. Human sin and evil, rooted in God-playing, impact the flow of history and the status of the covenant. Noah is commissioned by God to build an Ark. The Ark is to be filled with two of every kind of species. Once everyone is onboard, the rains begin. A flood covers the face of the earth. Only Noah and his descendants remain to carry on the human race and human faith. God makes a covenant with Noah. God promises never again to send a flood to kill all the creatures of the earth. The rainbow will be the sign of that covenant, a sign that the sun will shine again.

This story is a magnificent mix of grace with judgment. In the actual covenant made between God and Noah (Genesis 9:18–17), we learn that humankind owes its existence to a gracious God. There is no reason that God chooses to save Noah and his descendents other than God's pure love for the Creation.

The Tower of Babel

> Let's build a great city with a tower that reaches to the skies—a monument to our greatness! This will bring us together and keep us from scattering all over the world.
>
> —Genesis 11:4

The story of the Tower of Babel is the ultimate story of the human desire to play God. It is the tale of a people who decide to build a tower on the plain of Babylonia. The people want the tower to be tall enough to reach the sky so they can be face to face with God. God becomes furious with this grand demonstration of human pride and demolishes the tower.

God is also conscious of the great dangers of such pride when expressed by a community unified by language. Therefore, God confuses their speech. Without an understanding of one another, the community loses its power. The word *Babel* is similar to the Hebrew term for "confusion."

A Bad Word

The Tower of Babel and the ladder of success are both built with arrogance and pride. Both are efforts to play God. Both lead to the same place—away from God.

The Covenant with Abraham

> Then the Lord told Abraham, "Leave your country, your relatives, and your father's house, and go to the land I will show you. I will cause you to become the father of a great nation. I will bless you and make you famous, and I will make you a blessing to others. I will bless those who bless you and curse those who curse you. All the families of the earth will be blessed through you."
>
> —Genesis 12:1–3

God asks Abraham to take a huge risk. If Abraham is to follow God's wishes, he must first give up the security of family, friends, and homeland. This is a consistent biblical message. God tests human faith by demanding we first surrender what we hold most dear. God demands a choice, usually an excruciatingly difficult choice: security and safety vs. faith.

Abraham has been called to be the Father of the Jews. He is promised a life filled with blessings. Blessings and curses becomes another major theme of Hebrew Scripture. Those who follow God's plans will be rewarded with blessings. Those who disregard the will of God will suffer his curses. Again, God is active in history. God is judge of that history.

The Good Word

Faith demands maturation. Maturation means growth. Growth is change. Change is always risky. Change is the risk of following God where *he* leads us, not where *we* wish to go. It is not a choice easily or often made.

The Book of Genesis documents the further expansion of God's covenant with Abraham:

- God tells Abraham the actual borders of the land he will rule. (Genesis 15:18–21)

- Abraham is instructed that he and all male Jews must be circumcised. Circumcision will serve as a sign of the covenant. (God has a nasty habit of using pain as a sign of faith. Ouch!) (Genesis 17:9–14)

- Abraham is severely tested by God. God asks Abraham to sacrifice his son, Isaac, as witness to his faith in God's will. Abraham passes the test. Fortunately for Isaac, God stops the test before completion. For having passed this bitter test, God promises Abraham that his blessings will be multiplied. (Genesis 22:15–18)

If the story of Abraham being asked to prove his faith by sacrificing his son Isaac is not a metaphor, then it puts God in a very dark light for me. As a metaphor, I can relate to the idea that our faith must remain true, no matter how life tests us—and there could be no greater test than the loss of a child.

The Covenant with Isaac

The Lord appeared to him there and said, "Do not go to Egypt. Do as I say, and stay here in this land. If you do, I will be with you and bless you. I will give all this land to you and your descendants, just as I solemnly promised Abraham your father. I will cause your descendants to become as numerous as the stars, and I will give them all these lands. And through your descendants all the nations of the earth will be blessed. I will do this because Abraham listened to me and obeyed all my requirements, commands, regulations, and laws."

—Genesis 26:2–5

Isaac is the miracle child born to Abraham and Sarah when both parents were well past 90. (I said it was a miracle!) This would make Isaac the first descendant in fulfillment of God's promise to Abraham. The covenant God makes with Isaac further reveals the nature of covenantal relationship:

- Isaac must do as God says. Covenants are built on obedience.
- Blessings will be the reward for such obedience.
- Blessings are often associated with the multiplying of descendants.
- The covenant offered to Isaac is a direct result of his father's obedience.
- The covenant first made with Abraham is now being passed on to the son.
- Abraham's fulfillment of his vows was total. The same will be expected of Isaac.
- There is no such thing is a halfway covenant.

I remind my youth group that they are already building their personal legacy. Their behavior and actions now are forming the legacy they will be passing on to their children, should they choose to have them. It is a sobering thought to recognize that each and every day we are constructing a piece of that legacy. Think about it!

The Covenant with Jacob

The concept of covenant as legacy is further clarified in the haunting story of Jacob. Jacob actually tricks his old and almost blind father, Isaac, into believing he is his brother Esau. Rebekah, Jacob and Esau's mother, is fully engaged in the plot. Clearly, Rebekah sees

Jacob as the favored son and connives with him to win his father's blessing. Unaware of the deceit, Isaac blesses Jacob—the passing on of the covenant.

Jacob is the third link in the Abrahamic line of God's plan to build a nation. The story of how Jacob grabbed his brother Esau's birthright and blessing is a strange tale. On one hand, it seems to affirm trickery and deceit as a means to get what he wanted. On the other hand, it may be seen as a reward for determination and shrewdness.

I believe it is merely an acknowledgment that God chose Jacob to be the father of the 12 tribes of Israel. (God will choose who God wants!) This is why Isaac is unable to take back the blessing once it has been given. Even when made aware of his mistake, Isaac must accept that the blessing had passed to God's choice. The blessing is not Isaac's possession; it is God's.

Abraham, Isaac, and Jacob are among the most significant people of Hebrew Scripture. Their significance, however, is not so much about their personal character as it is about the character of God. They were heroes, yes, but also flawed human beings. They were known to lie, cheat, and be enormously selfish. God does not choose perfect creatures to execute his plans; he chooses very *human* beings.

In a Word or Two

Show me a hero and I will write you a tragedy.

—F. Scott Fitzgerald, *The Crack-Up* (1945)

The Story of Joseph

Joseph's amazing story is captured in Genesis 30–50. Let me capture the highlights of this great saga:

- Joseph is the son of Jacob. He had 10 older brothers.

- Joseph was his father's favorite and functioned like a spoiled brat.

- Joseph was annoyingly overconfident.

- His brothers conspire to be rid of him and dump him into a pit.

- Unbeknownst to his brothers, Joseph is retrieved from the pit and taken to Egypt.

- In Egypt he is made a slave and spends time in prison.

- His *accurate* reading of dreams grabs the attention of the Pharoah.

- The Pharoah elevates Joseph to the role of right-hand man.

- Joseph accurately predicts a famine and has his nation well-prepared. This same famine brings his hungry brothers to grovel at his feet.

- The brothers beg to be forgiven.

- Joseph tells them to stop begging. He is not God. Of course they are forgiven.

The story of Joseph is also about relationships. It is a story of intense sibling rivalry and of a father showing one child too much love over the others. It is also a story of how Joseph found his faith, his humility, and his heart at the bottom of a well. At times we have to hit bottom to know that we are not God.

The Least You Need to Know

- The Creation is God's ultimate expression of covenant.

- The great Flood is God's judgment mixed with grace.

- The Tower of Babel displays the human desire to play God.

- Abraham is the father of the Jewish people. God's covenant with Abraham is one that promises blessings for obedience and curses for disobedience.

- Abraham's legacy is passed to his son, Isaac, who then passes it on to his son Jacob.

- Joseph finds his soul in the bottom of a well.

Chapter 4

The Exodus

In This Chapter

- Jacob's descendants are forced into slavery
- God delivers the Jews from the Egyptian bondage
- War between the Pharaoh and the God of the Hebrews
- Moses leads the Hebrews out of Egypt on a perilous journey through the wilderness
- Moses receives the Law

Can you imagine being a slave? Can you fathom the idea of being owned by another human being? Can you comprehend what must go on in the minds of those who think of themselves as masters? Absurd as it may seem, slavery is historically a common phenomena sanctioned by people of supposed faith in God. Our own nation has a history dripping with the blood, sweat, and tears of slaves. The history of the oppression of the Hebrew people is one of the great tragedies of history. Their story is one of a constant battle for freedom and the right to believe. The atrocities they have suffered at the hands of so-called God-fearing folks remains a faith-paralyzing puzzle.

As you read this chapter, you will come to see why both Moses and the Exodus are at the core of Hebrew faith. The Egyptian bondage was the low point of Hebrew history. The exodus to freedom, led by Moses, the high point. It is also *the* turning point. All Hebrew history will pivot on this event. There is no going back. They must never be slaves again. Freedom becomes the foundation upon which Hebrew faith is built.

Moses

In Genesis we heard of the Hebrew migration to Egypt. Jacob and his sons come to Egypt in search of food. Joseph serves in the Pharaoh's court. The Hebrew population multiplies over the years, and soon becomes a major threat to the Egyptians. The Pharaoh enslaves the Hebrews and forces them into hard labor. The Hebrew people are used to perform fieldwork and to build the store-cities of Pithom and Raamses.

The Pharaoh's plan does not succeed. The Hebrew population continues to grow. A new and brutal plan is conceived. He orders the midwives to kill all newborn Hebrew boy babies at birth. The midwives manage to get out of this gruesome scheme by telling the Pharaoh that the Hebrew women give birth before they could get to them. Then the Pharaoh commands that all Hebrew boy babies be cast into the Nile River. Moses is born while this edict is in force.

Moses was the third son of Leah and Jacob. He was born a Levite. Levites were intended to serve God and the people as priests. Moses is saved from the Pharaoh's decree of death by the wisdom of his mother. She prepares a waterproof basket for him and sails him down river toward the palace of the Pharaoh. The Pharaoh's daughter discovers the basket and the baby Moses and decides to keep him, knowing he is a Hebrew child. One of the great ironies of this story is that the Pharaoh's daughter hires Moses' real mother to nurse her own child. Although Moses is raised as the son of the Pharaoh's daughter, we are led to believe that Moses is aware of his heritage as a Hebrew. This identification with his own people is clearly demonstrated when Moses murders an Egyptian he witnesses beating a Hebrew slave. Moses then flees to Midian.

The Good Word

God chose a murderer to lead his people out of Egyptian bondage. Once again we see that God does not make choices on the basis of human character. God's decisions are an expression of God's will.

Moses builds a home and a family in this foreign land. He becomes a shepherd. The life of a shepherd is lonely. It could be said that this nomadic existence served to heighten his spiritual sensitivity. As God prepares Moses for a call to leadership …

- The Pharaoh who has sought to kill Moses dies.
- The agony of the Hebrew people has intensified. The oppression has grown even more severe.
- The cry of the Hebrew people is said to be heard by God.

Moses becomes God's instrument of deliverance. Moses meets God on Mount Sinai, a mountain considered sacred in ancient times. On the mountain he encounters a burning bush. In the Bible, fire was often associated with the presence of God. In the modern sense— Moses saw the light.

Moses is not eager to accept the call of God. He raises these five objections:

- I am a nobody.
- I will not be able to explain the message.
- The Hebrew people will not believe me.
- I am afraid of public speaking.
- I have a better idea: Send somebody else.

Moses is so human. Can't you identify with his response? I love the fact that God's chosen leaders usually want to run the other way. At this point Moses returns to Egypt.

Let My People Go!

Moses and his brother, Aaron, are finally accepted by the elders of the Hebrew people. They have their first encounter with the Pharaoh and tell him of God's command. Moses and Aaron tell the Pharaoh to let the Hebrew people go. But because the Pharaoh does not know their God, he has zero respect for the authority of this command. He rejects the request. The Pharaoh also makes the burden of the slaves even more difficult. He instructs the taskmasters to require the slaves to find the straw needed to make the bricks.

What happens next is a miracle—an event I cannot hope to explain. As a sign to the Pharaoh of the power of God, Moses' staff is said to become a snake. The Pharaoh calls in his wise men and magicians, who then turn their staffs into snakes. Moses' snake is said to have devoured these other snakes. The Pharaoh remains unimpressed.

Moses next predicts the plagues. He warns the Pharaoh of God's wrath. God is furious with the Pharaoh for enslaving his people and keeping them from worship. The plagues arrive as follows:

- Aaron strikes the Nile with his rod, and the river turns to blood. Since the Egyptians worshipped the Nile River, this plague was seen to show the overwhelming power of the Hebrew God. Hapi, the Egyptian god of the Nile, is defeated.

- The next plague is frogs. Frogs can be horrid pests, and the plague of frogs is so fierce that the Pharaoh asks Moses and Aaron to pray to their God to remove it.

- A plague of gnats arrives unannounced. The Egyptian wise men are unable to arrest the plague. Even the Egyptian sorcerers point to the finger of God as the culprit in bringing on this plague.

- Moses next tells the Pharaoh that there will be a plague of flies. The flies will be choosy. The flies will only plague the land of the Egyptians. The land of Goshen, where the Hebrews live, will remain fly-free. The Pharaoh hates flies; they drive him nuts. Again the Pharaoh asks Moses to intercede.

- The Pharaoh is warned that there will be a cattle epidemic. Again only Egyptian cattle are affected.

- A plague of boils and sores affects the people and animals of Egypt. Moses is held responsible for this plague. It is believed that his tossing of pottery-kiln soot into the air was the symbolic cause of the plague.

- God warns the Pharaoh that his disobedience will be used to teach others a lesson. A savage hailstorm strikes Egypt, leaving the land of Goshen untouched. Even some of the Pharaoh's servants heed Moses' warning and go into hiding during the storm.

- The eighth plague is a swarm of locusts. The Pharaoh agrees to let only the Hebrew men go. Moses and Aaron turn this offer down. The Pharaoh is wilting under the pressure of the plagues, and he asks to be forgiven! The locusts are blown away.

- One of the chief gods of the Egyptians was the sun. So when the plague of darkness arrives unannounced, the God of the Hebrews proves his power. The Pharaoh allows everyone to leave except the flocks and herds. Moses declines the offer, and the Pharaoh is furious.

- Moses announces the final plague. All the firstborn of Egypt will die at the word of the Lord. God will once again choose to spare the Hebrews, passing over the houses marked as Hebrew. To identify the homes as Hebrew, the blood of a sacrificial lamb is painted on the doorposts and upper beam of door frames. This event is the establishment of Passover, marking a new beginning for the Hebrew people. They are now free. The Exodus is to be seen as the day their history begins.

Moses does see the Pharaoh one more time. The Pharaoh has had more than enough proof of the power of the Hebrew God. The Pharaoh not only grants freedom for the Hebrews to leave, he also asks for a blessing from Moses. The owners of slaves are instructed to give farewell gifts of food, coins, agricultural implements, blankets, or bolts of cloth. These gifts will help the Hebrews remember Egypt in a more positive light. Clearly the Egyptians are wary of the power of the Hebrew God.

Exit Stage Right

The actual Exodus out of Egypt is dated about 1450 B.C. The Hebrew people believed themselves to be divinely guided. They had faith that God would lead their exit out of Egypt. God is thought to avoid the more direct route through the land of the Philistines and instead takes the Hebrews via the wilderness toward the Red Sea.

The *Red Sea* means "sea of reeds" in Hebrew. This portion of the sea probably refers to a series of swamps and lakes. It is here that the Hebrews make camp. The Pharaoh has already changed his mind and is now actively pursuing his former slaves. The Egyptians are said to be traveling in 600 chariots. The Hebrews are aware that the Egyptians are in hot pursuit, and Moses reassures them that God will continue to guide and deliver them.

Faith history records the events as follows:

- The Hebrews are camped in terror.
- Moses leads his people in prayer and worship.
- Moses raises his staff, and the sea is said to part. This may actually have been the tidal movement of the water.
- The Hebrews travel on foot and are able to cross the riverbed.
- The Egyptians follow on chariot and get hopelessly mired in the mud.
- The waters return, and the Egyptians are drowned.
- Egypt and the Pharaoh are defeated.

From the plagues to the parting of the Red Sea, the predominant theme is that God is actively involved in freeing the Hebrews.

Yes, one could argue that all these events are both natural and coincidence. Faith, of course, leads one to a different conclusion: that God was on the Hebrews' side. I think even the Pharaoh came to believe that.

Imagine the position of the Hebrews. Moses tells the Pharaoh that God will send plagues. They watch the frogs, gnats, and locust arrive. They watch the Egyptians lose their cattle and get blasted by hail, while they stay safe and sound in untouched Goshen. Then they finally leave Egypt, only to be trailed by the Pharaoh's army. They wind up at the Red Sea, which Moses manages to make passable. The Egyptian charioteers get stuck in the mud and the waters return, drowning the Pharaoh's troops. Is it any wonder that the Hebrews believed that God was on their side? Should we be shocked that the Hebrews saw themselves as God's chosen people?

The First Outward-Bound Program

The Hebrews walk on into the wilderness, bloated with confidence. They have just experienced a major victory at the Red Sea. Moses appears to be a fearless and visionary leader. With God at the helm, how can they miss getting to the Promised Land?

Still, the trip proves difficult. There are several crises. These crises are used by God as a time of testing:

- **Finding water in the wilderness (Exodus 15:22–27).** The wilderness is mostly desert. The Hebrews are often without water, and the only water they do find is bitter. God gives them a shrub to put into the water to sweeten it, and God quenches the Hebrew's thirst.

- **Finding food in the wilderness (Exodus 16:1–26).** The food that the Hebrews find to eat in the desert is called manna. Basically, manna is bug poop left on the leaves of shrubs—not exactly a gourmet feast, but enough protein to survive. Once again the Hebrews claim the hand of God in their survival.

- **Water flows from a rock (Exodus 17:1–7).** The Hebrews are losing faith, especially in Moses. They are literally dying of thirst. Moses fears for his own life, suspecting that if they don't find water soon, his own people will stone him to death. Once again Moses raises his shepherd's staff (sort of the original magic wand) and water flows from the rock. God and Moses pass this fierce test. This may have been a natural event, but to the eyes of faith, it was further testimony that God was protecting his chosen people.

- **Battling the Amalekites (Exodus 17:8–16).** The Hebrews were not a warring tribe, but the Amalekites were a group of desert nomads and warriors. Moses asks Aaron to form an army to fight the Amalekites. The Hebrews win the battle. The only people more stunned than the Amalekites by this victory are the Hebrews.

To the eyes of faith, the passing of each of these tests offers further proof that God is providing for the needs of the Hebrew people. God provided an oasis when needed. God brought victory over a nomadic tribe. God even brought Jethro, a man who was comfortable and familiar with the desert, to offer advice on how to make daily living easier. (Jethro's visit is found in Exodus 18:1–27.)

In good times and in bad, on top of the mountain and in the pits of despair, the God of the Hebrews is there. In times of great difficulty, the Hebrews are taught to trust, not test, their God.

The Ten Commandments Are Not Multiple Choice

Chapters 19 and 20 of Exodus form the heart of the Hebrew Scripture. It is here that God declares a covenant with the Hebrew people. God wants a special relationship with his people.

The Ten Commandments form the core of this covenant and relationship.

The following Ten Commandments are quoted directly from the *Life Application Study Bible, New Living Translation* (Tundale House Publishers, Inc.), Exodus 20:1–17:

> Then God instructed the people as follows. I am the Lord your God, who rescued you from slavery in Egypt.
>
> 1. Do not worship any other gods beside me.
>
> 2. Do not make idols of any kind, whether in the shape of birds or animals or fish. You must never worship or bow down to them, for I, the Lord your God am a jealous God who will not share your affection with any other god! I do not leave unpunished the sins of those who

hate me, but I punish the children for the sins of their
parents to the third and fourth generations. But I lavish
my love on those who love me and obey my commands,
even for a thousand generations.

3. Do not misuse the name of the Lord your God. The
   Lord will not let you go unpunished if you misuse his
   name.

4. Remember to observe the Sabbath day by keeping it
   holy. Six days a week are set apart for your daily duties
   and regular work, but the seventh day is a day of rest
   dedicated to the Lord your God. On that day no one in
   your household may do any kind of work. This includes
   you, your sons and daughters, your male and female servants, your livestock, and any foreigners living among
   you. For in six days the Lord made the heavens, the
   earth, the sea, and everything in them; then he rested on
   the seventh day. That is why the Lord blessed the
   Sabbath day and set it apart as holy.

5. Honor your father and mother. Then you will live a
   long, full life in the land your Lord your God will give
   you.

6. Do not murder.

7. Do not commit adultery.

8. Do not steal.

9. Do not testify falsely against your neighbor.

10. Do not covet your neighbor's house. Do not covet your
    neighbor's wife, male or female servant, ox or donkey, or
    anything else your neighbor owns.

Moses serves as the mediator of the Ten Commandments. It is
Moses who receives them, offers them to his people, and teaches
and instructs about them. Moses returns to the mountain to receive
the Covenant Code.

These are the "case laws" that will be used to govern in particular
situations. These case laws are aimed at addressing the kinds of issues that are bound to occur in a community. There are laws concerning the altar, slaves, offenses that require the death penalty,

bodily injuries and property damage, as well the requirement of equal treatment for rich or poor, Israelite or stranger.

The Law received by Moses was intended to accomplish the following:

- To make clear the unique relationship between God and the Hebrews
- To offer rules that do not enslave the soul but instead grant true spiritual freedom
- To offer a way of life that is holy and acceptable to God
- To offer a code of conduct that would enable the Hebrew people to live in a manner befitting their chosen status
- To remind the Hebrews that holy living must be lived on a daily basis

In a Word or Two

Freedom is the oxygen of the soul.

—Moshe Dayan

We are in bondage to the law in order that we may be free.

—Cicero

The function of freedom is to free somebody else.

—Toni Morrison

A Lot of Bull

The wandering was thought to have lasted 40 years—or one heck of a long time. Needless to say, the Hebrew people have grown restless. They are questioning the leadership of Moses as well as their departure from Egypt. Slaves or not, they at least knew exactly where they were, who they were, and what was expected of them. In the wilderness they experience tremendous anxiety. Will we ever get to the Promised Land? Is God still on our side? Has he abandoned us?

As is often the case in times of great anxiety, the Hebrews lost faith. The Hebrews remember how the Egyptians worshipped a god named Apis, which was an idol shaped like a young bull. The Hebrews create such a bull from melted gold and an altar is constructed from fieldstones. After eating and drinking, the Hebrews engage in wild party behavior. They begin to live and act as if there is no tomorrow—no hope. The Hebrew people have shattered the covenant.

While all this is happening, Moses is atop the mountain. When he returns and sees the wild dancing and sexual behavior, as well as the golden bull, he is enraged. He smashes the stone tablets God gave him that hold the Law. He destroys and burns the bull idol, scatters the residue on the water, and forces the Hebrews to drink the tainted water. The Hebrews are literally forced to swallow their false worship.

Leviticus, Numbers, and Deuteronomy

The remainder of the Torah (the first five books of the Bible) consists of Leviticus, Numbers, and Deuteronomy. Leviticus is set at the base of Mount Sinai. The book is filled with instructions on the use of the tabernacle. The tabernacle was believed to be God's dwelling place, a sanctuary to be used for worship, the sacred space of atonement. Leviticus contains extensive and detailed information on how to live a holy life.

Though the book is said to be written by Moses, it is clearly shaped by priestly editors—the P source. Leviticus focuses on the importance of the priestly family, the Levites. Leviticus outlines a strict discipline of behavior as well as regulations for rituals. Both are intended to keep the Hebrew people in line, so that they might never again break the covenant as they did in their worship of the golden bull.

Numbers is the fourth book in the series—"The Five Books of Moses." *Numbers* in Hebrew means "in the wilderness." The book has three distinct sections:

- The Hebrews get ready to depart from Mount Sinai. (Chapters 1–10)

- The Hebrews travel to Kadesh. (Chapters 11–21)

- The Hebrews approach Canaan—the Promised Land. (Chapters 22–36)

Numbers covers events while the Hebrews wandered in the wilderness. The book deals with the Hebrews' wavering support for Moses, as well as their ultimate breaking of the Covenant. Though the book details God's ongoing involvement in his people's lives, it stresses the growing evidence of the Hebrews' lack of faith.

Deuteronomy takes up where Numbers leaves off. The Hebrew people are camped in Moab and await the opportunity to conquer Canaan. (Canaan is the Promised Land. They believe God has bequeathed Canaan to them.) To get to Canaan they must cross the Jordan River. Moses is aware that he is dying and that he will not get to cross the river. Moses wants to have one more chance to teach his people, a final chance to preach—the last word.

Moses delivers three sermons:

- Sermon One reviews all the events of the Exodus and the wilderness. He documents how actively God has been true to the covenant he has made with the Hebrews. (Chapters 1–4)

- Sermon Two reviews the Ten Commandments and the moral expectations of the Law. (Chapters 5–6)

- Sermon Three describes how the Hebrews are to live holy lives within the holy land. (Chapters 7–30)

The final four chapters of Deuteronomy are dedicated to the final days of Moses. Moses never sets foot on the Promised Land.

Exodus as Spiritual Paradigm

A paradigm is a model. The Exodus is a model for the journey of spirituality. I find 10 vital lessons for spiritual growth and freedom offered in the model of the Hebrew exodus from Egypt:

- Even the most faithful can become enslaved.

- What enslaves you keeps you from worship.

- Slavery can become comfortable, safe, and secure.

- The movement to spiritual freedom requires leadership.

- The movement to spiritual freedom requires risk.

- True spiritual freedom takes time to find.

- True spiritual freedom demands passing many tests of maturity.

- The journey to spiritual freedom will often lead to dead ends.

- There will be many along the way who will try to lead you back to Egypt.

- The spiritual journey to freedom is costly, but the prize that is won—your soul—is worth it.

The Least You Need to Know

- God called Moses to lead the Hebrews out of Egyptian bondage.

- Moses tells the Pharaoh to let his people go.

- The Pharaoh refuses to heed Moses' warnings of coming plagues.

- The final plague is the death of the firstborn Egyptian children. The Hebrew firstborn are passed over by the angel of death.

- Passover marks the central importance of the Exodus to Hebrew history and Scripture.

- Moses receives the Law on Mount Sinai. The Law is intended to hold the Hebrew people together during the wandering in the wilderness—a true test of faith.

- Though the covenant of the Law is broken in worship of the golden bull, Moses restores order and faith.

Chapter **5**

The Judges

In This Chapter

- Joshua is the successor to Moses
- Joshua leads the invasion and conquering of Canaan
- Joshua 24 deals with the establishment of a Tribal Confederacy
- The Hebrews must deal with the temptations of Canaanite culture
- Twelve judges rule for a span of 410 years
- Samuel is the last judge of the Hebrews and the greatest spiritual leader since Moses

When I first imagined the arrival of the wandering Hebrews to the Promised Land, my vision was pretty idyllic. I pictured weary men, women, and children trudging out of the desert into a land as green as Ireland. In my mind Canaan was a country laced by sparkling brooks, a place where there was always plenty to eat, a holy ground where roots went in easy and deep.

I also assumed that they walked in unannounced, set up camp on the verdant hills, and established a simple life of pastoral bliss.

I reckoned that their arrival was peaceful and that the land of Canaan welcomed them with open arms. I believed that the Hebrews must have known daily joy—God had fulfilled his promise; this fertile soil was now their own. Wow, was I wrong!

As you read this chapter, you will learn of Joshua, the successor to Moses, and the holy war he led to conquer Canaan. You will hear of the Tribal Confederacy and the judges who governed for 410 years. You will learn why the judges were selected and why the Hebrew people resisted being ruled by a king. You will come to know Samuel, the last and greatest judge, and realize why he would finally relent and name a king.

Joshua

There is really no information as to who Joshua was or why he was chosen to be Moses' successor. Obviously, he was a great military leader, and certainly he was a man of significant charisma. Other than that, we know next to nothing, except the history contained in the Biblical book that bears his name.

The Book of Deuteronomy ends with the death of Moses. Tragically, Moses never gets to set foot on the sacred soil of the Promised Land. Now the job of leading the Hebrews fell to Joshua. Suffice it to say, Moses was no easy act to follow.

In the first verses of the Book of Joshua, Joshua is told that this chunk of the Fertile Crescent will be Israel's on one condition: The Law must be obeyed and studied with discipline.

Obedience to God's commands would yield victory and prosperity. Disobedience would bring only judgment, suffering, and failure. A neat and tidy doctrine of blessings and curses would govern their lives in the Promised Land.

Like an America already inhabited by tribes of Indians, the Promised Land was home to many native Canaanite tribes. The first 12 chapters of the Book of Joshua document the invasion and conquering of Canaan. Joshua led the Hebrews on three swift and victorious campaigns. Joshua masterminded a strategy of invasion that led the Hebrews first to conquer central Canaan as far as Shechem. A second thrust captured the southern hill country and a final attack seized the northern hill country. Joshua had led the Hebrews to total victory.

Spread the Good Word

After the death of Moses the Lord's servant, the Lord spoke to Joshua son of Nun, Moses' assistant. "Now that my servant Moses is dead, you must lead my people across the Jordan River into the land that I am giving them."

—Joshua 1:1–2

These three blitzes were bloody and savage. They were conducted with religious fervor. Think of them as a "holy war"—the very worst kind of war. No prisoners were taken. No spoils divided.

The fact that the conquest of Canaan was so savage is a disturbing aspect of Hebrew history. I do think it foreshadows the position of Israel today, which is to speak from a position of strength. Had Israel experienced a terrorist attack of the magnitude of that in New York City and the Pentagon on September 11, 2001, they would have responded swiftly and with great force. No caution. No coalition-building. Israel would have felt spiritually justified in any action it chose to take.

Remember, the history of the Hebrew people is one which sees God actively engaged in wars. God is not neutral in Hebrew Scripture; God takes a side. Though at times God takes the side of the enemy, to teach Israel a lesson, most often God is thought to be squarely on the side of his people.

Everything that would burn was put to the torch. The battle at Gibeon was a massacre. Five Amorite kings went up against Joshua. The Hebrews attacked at dawn. The Amorites were blinded by the early morning light. They panicked, and the slaughter was on. The five kings were left swaying from the branches of trees. The invasion and conquering of Canaan was anything but pretty!

The Tribal Confederacy

Chapter 24 of the Book of Joshua is one of the most significant in Hebrew Scriptures. Joshua's farewell address is found in Chapter 23. It is in Chapter 24 that we hear of a great convocation at Shechem, a city located near the grave of Joseph.

It was here that Joshua challenged the Hebrews to choose whom they would serve. Would they reconfirm their covenant with God, or would they choose instead to worship the gods of the Canaanites?

It was at this assembly that the Hebrews were organized into 12 tribes. Each tribe had considerable autonomy but remained spiritually bonded to the other 11 through their covenant with God. The Tribal Confederacy established at Shechem was more religious in nature than political. In times of military emergency, however, the tribes agreed to band together to fight the common foe. The Confederacy also served to unite the tribes by language, customs, and the care of a central sanctuary.

The Good Word

Shechem was an important fortress and also a major religious center. In the acropolis stood a large temple. The temple of Baal-Berith would become the first center of the Tribal Confederacy.

The glue that truly held the 12 tribes together was the belief that God continued to act on behalf of his people.

The 12 tribes that gathered at Shechem came there to remember how God led them out of Egypt, provided manna for them in the wilderness, bestowed the Law upon Moses, and brought the Hebrews successfully to the Promised Land. The Confederacy was rooted in the belief that God was on their side, that the covenant must remain strong, and that all foreign gods must be rejected.

It is the renewal of this covenant at Shechem that gives rise to the use of the term *Israel*. Israel is primarily a religious word. Not all Hebrews are Israelites. The only true Israelites are those who have once again affirmed that God is their God, and they his people.

Battling Baal

The Law of Israel was covenant law. It was not secular or civil. It was 100 percent religious. This law held that all of life was to be governed by God's wishes and demands. The Israelites were to be at all times and in all places accountable to God. This belief in total accountability led to a rapid expansion of the Law. The Law was adapted to a new agricultural lifestyle. During the period of the Tribal Confederacy, Israel also borrowed many laws from the culture of the Fertile Crescent.

Israelite life was crude by comparison to that of the Canaanites'. The Canaanite culture was far more sophisticated and aristocratic. The Israelites were semi-nomads coming out of a desert background. They found the Canaanite culture foreign and offensive. The Israelites became farmers, their lives dominated by the tilling of the soil and the planting of crops.

The Good Word

The followers of the Baal religion also believed in temple prostitution. It was thought that human couplings could ignite Baal and Balaath, encouraging these gods to sexually mate. Thus, the revival of nature was linked directly to sexual intercourse. Sex was elevated to the realm of the divine.

God had proven that he was the God of history. Now God would have to contend with the gods of nature. The gods of the Fertile Crescent claimed control of rainfall, fertility, and the cycle of the seasons. The Baal religion was of the belief that when Baal, the male deity, would have sexual intercourse with Balaath, the female partner, the soil would become fertile and yield a rich harvest of crops.

The gods of the Fertile Crescent were practical. They were thought to control those forces of nature that had the most direct impact on the daily lives of the Israelites. You can imagine how tempting it was to pledge allegiance to a god that promised rain and a good harvest, if that harvest meant your livelihood, health, and happiness. This, coupled with the obvious appeal of sexy gods, made for a tough spiritual opponent for God.

12 for 410

Twelve judges ruled the Tribal Confederacy for a span of 410 years. Judges were not like kings. The office of judge was nonhereditary. Judges were selected by virtue of their charisma, which is a strong and obvious spiritual presence; a sense that the individual is uniquely gifted by God to hold a special role; a person who is un- commonly spiritually attractive to others; a natural-born leader.

This charisma was noticeable not only to the members of a judge's clan, but to surrounding tribes as well. Judges were witnessed as being shrewd in battle and wise in the interpretation of the Law. Great physical prowess also encouraged a strong following.

Spread the Good Word

Then the Spirit of the Lord took possession of Gideon. He blew a ram's horn as a call to arms, and the men of the Abiezer came to him. He also sent messengers throughout Mannaseh, Asher, Zebulun, and Naphtali, summoning their warriors, and all of them responded.

—Judges 6:34–35

Three of the best-known judges were ...

- Samson, the Incredible Hulk of his time. The legend of Samson's great physical strength is attributed to his being empowered by the spirit of God. Samson was not a military leader—unusual for a judge. His tragic demise was the direct result of God-playing. (Judges 14:6)

  Samson is best known for his mythic encounter with Delilah. Delilah is said to have removed Samson's extraordinary power by cutting off his hair. She is thought to have left Samson looking like Mr. Clean. Hairless, Samson was pretty much a wimp. I think the moral of the story is that Samson lost his heart to Delilah, and in so doing, he lost his will, his source of strength.

- Gideon, best known for turning down the Israelite invitation to be king. He saw God as the only true ruler. It was Gideon who orchestrated the defeat of the Midianites, a group of camel-riding nomads who had threatened to drive the Israelites into the hills. (Judges 6:5)

- Deborah, Israel's only woman judge. Deborah called on a general named Barak to do battle with the Canaanite forces led by a general named Sisera. Deborah correctly predicted that Barak would win the battle and that Sisera would be killed by a woman—which he was, her name was Jael. (Judges 4–5)

Each of these judges helped to hold the Confederacy together. Each was charged with the settling of many legal disputes. It was the function of the judge to keep the tribes focused on the Law and convinced of the charismatic presence of God in their lives.

Uncle Samuel

The 12 tribes of Israel were bound together by a common faith, not a centralized government. As time passed, it became obvious that the Confederacy was no longer effective in addressing the troubles the tribes faced in Canaan. The Confederacy, in fact, encouraged each tribe to be independent.

The first effort to establish a centralized government took place at Shechem, the same place where the Confederacy had been established during the time of Joshua. Gideon, a great military champion, was invited to serve as king. Israel would then be ruled by a monarch, and such rule would be passed on by heredity. Gideon flatly refused the invitation.

It was Samuel, the last great judge of Israel, who not only led a religious revival but also set the stage for the establishment of a monarchy. Samuel was without question the greatest spiritual leader since Moses. His charisma was unquestioned, his wisdom powerful and evident.

Samuel had abundant anxiety about the anointing of a king. He, like Gideon, believed that God was the sole ruler and that the concept of a king granted too much power to a human being. Samuel was forced to accept that his own sons were unsuited to the task. Samuel finally relented and anointed Saul as Israel's first king. No longer would Israel be only a people now they would become a nation.

Spread the Good Word

Finally, the leaders of Israel met at Ramah to discuss the matter with Samuel. "Look," they told him, "you are old, and your sons are not like you. Give us a king like all the other nations have." Samuel was very upset with their request and went to the Lord for advice. "Do as they say," the Lord replied, "for it is me they are rejecting, not you. They don't want me to be their king any longer. Ever since I brought them from Egypt they have continually forsaken me and followed other gods. And now they are giving you the same treatment. Do as they ask, but solemnly warn them about how a king will treat them."

—1 Samuel 8:4–9

The books of Joshua and Judges are not simple books. They are, however, important books with a vital spiritual message. Here are some of the major points made in these two books:

- Disobedience to God would have dire consequences.
- The nation of Israel was only loosely organized as a Tribal Confederacy.
- This Tribal Confederacy was ruled by charismatic Judges.
- Israel spiritually struggled with the religions of the Fertile Crescent. Superstition was on the rise, and sexual immorality became widespread.
- Israel was often at war with the Philistines, the Moabites, and the Midianites.
- The 12 tribes of Israel periodically met at a central sanctuary, including Shiloh, Bethel, Gilgal, and Mizpah.
- Israel often fell into gross idolatry.
- God remained faithful.

I must admit that both Joshua and Judges appear to show God as an advocate of extreme violence. I struggle mightily with that perspective. Whatever the reason, both books see God as solely on Israel's side. In fact, God is presumed to share in their hatred of enemies. The notion of a hating God is impossible for me to swallow.

The Least You Need to Know

- Joshua led a brutal but successful invasion and conquering of Canaan.
- A Tribal Confederacy was formed at Shechem.
- The Tribal Confederacy was composed of 12 tribes united by a common covenant with God.
- The Tribal Confederacy was ruled by charismatic and inspirational judges.
- The Israelites were challenged by the religions of the Fertile Crescent, as well as by several warring tribes—most noticeably the Philistines.

- The Confederacy began to weaken. The people called for a king.
- Samuel, the last great judge of Israel, reluctantly anointed Saul king.

Part 3

Hebrew Scripture: The Nation

It was Moses who led the Jewish people on the exodus out of Egypt on their long wandering in the desert. It was Moses who received the Law from God and established a covenant between God and his chosen people, the Hebrews. Scholars refer to this covenant as the Mosaic Covenant. This covenant, however, was established by God with all of his people. Though Moses serves as the mediator, his role concludes with the reception and delivery of the Law to his people.

As the Confederacy weakened, the need for a king became obvious. After Samuel anointed Saul the first king, the Hebrew people were well on their way to becoming a true nation. It was under David that their nationhood was both declared and truly celebrated.

As a nation the covenant with God made a dramatic shift. The king was not only the mediator of the covenant, but the interpreter of the Law as well. The king was seen as the keeper of faith. When the king spoke, God spoke. When the king acted, it was God moving among his people.

No longer just a people, the Hebrews had become a nation with a unique historical relationship to God. As a nation of favored status, chosen and designated by God, the Hebrew people believed that God was actively present in their political, economic, and social actions. God was no longer simply the God of the individual, the Hebrew people, but was now champion of the ambitions and dreams of a nation.

Chapter 6

The Kings

In This Chapter

- Philistine aggression strikes the final blow in the Tribal Confederacy
- Samuel reluctantly anoints Saul king
- Saul has a major dispute with the prophet Samuel and a bitter rivalry with David
- David becomes the next king and the true architect of the Israelite State
- King Solomon reigns in opulence and splendor

Samuel was the last great judge of the Tribal Confederacy. The final blow to the Confederacy was the aggression of the Philistine armies. It became clear, even to Samuel, that the 12 tribes of Israel needed a king to unite them. Samuel's fear was that a king came too close to a god; a warning he shared with the Hebrews on a regular basis. Still, without a great military champion to lead them and a king to unite them, the Hebrews faced defeat—even extinction. Samuel could see the writing on the wall. He recognized that even a God-playing king was better than a vanquished Israel.

Saul was anointed by Samuel as the first king of Israel. He was charismatic, had recorded numerous military victories, and had earned the confidence of the Israelites, who believed that Saul alone could rid them of the Philistine invaders.

As you read this chapter, you will discover how 12 tribes loosely gathered together as a Confederacy, ruled by judges, becomes a powerful nation governed by kings. You will come to know a good bit more about Saul, David, and Solomon, the three great kings of Israel, and how God-playing would be both their temptation and their downfall.

Saul the Sad

During Saul's reign as king, he had three significant enemies: the prophet Samuel, a young man named David, and himself. Saul was a victim of his own insecurity and jealousy. His life was uniquely tragic, as he was ultimately rejected by the old order, represented by Samuel, as well as by the new order, represented by David. Saul's rejection by Samuel was the result of a dispute over how to handle the spoils of war. Samuel believed in the rules of a holy war. He was convinced that God required taking and sacrificing all the Amalekite livestock. Saul, however, decided to sacrifice only the animals that were in bad shape and kept the cream of the crop for himself. Samuel was livid with Saul and turned his affections toward a young man named David, who had knocked out the Philistine version of Arnold Schwarzeneger, Goliath.

Saul had a real love-hate relationship with David. Saul was depressed by Samuel's assertion that God was through with him for good, and only the sweet music of David's lyre brought Saul any comfort. David became like a son to him. Their relationship turned sour when David's popularity skyrocketed at the same time Saul's was on a rapid decline. When Saul's own son Jonathan seemed to care more for David than for his own father, the bond was severed. Old Saul was fuming.

Saul's jealousy became rage, and that rage brought out wickedness in him. Saul urged his servants and his son to assassinate David. Jonathan told David of his father's plans and foiled the attempt. Saul remained tormented by the immense popularity of David and was deeply wounded by his son's "betrayal." While David was playing his lyre for him, Saul's jealousy erupted, and he hurled a spear at

David. David was forced to go on the run to avoid Saul's jealous wrath. Michal, Saul's daughter and David's wife, helped keep her husband safe. Again, Saul felt betrayed by his own flesh and blood.

Spread the Good Word

This was their song: "Saul has killed his thousands, and David his ten thousands!" This made Saul very angry. "What's this?" he said, "They credit David with ten thousands and me with only thousands. Next they'll be making him their king!" So from that time on Saul kept a jealous eye on David.

—1 Samuel 18:7–9

Jonathan must have been stunned by his father's horrid behavior. He must have been shocked to experience his father's gross insecurity and evil jealousy. It took great courage on Jonathan's part to reject his father's wishes and to remain true to his friendship with David. Jonathan's courage was rooted in following a law higher than his father's orders—the will of God.

Saul's Top and Bottom Ten

Saul's reign as Israel's first God-appointed king had some highlights and numerous lowlights. Saul's reign was a real roller-coaster ride in terms of his leadership and faith:

- Saul was a striking physical presence, known for his courage and generosity.
- Saul was a fierce warrior and an awesome military leader.
- Saul displayed great greed in keeping the spoils of war.
- Saul was rejected by Samuel.
- Samuel declared that God was fed up with Saul.

- Saul's jealousy for David was massive.

- Saul showed little spiritual depth or understanding; he was too often led by his passions and not his faith.

- Saul was guilty of attempted murder. He drove David out of Israel.

- Saul was a huge disappointment to his son Jonathan and his daughter Michal.

- Saul and Jonathan died tragically, which was recorded in a song by David in 2 Samuel.

The saga of Saul was a sad one: a man of commanding presence and potential, brought down by childish greed and jealousy.

David the Divine

David was adored, wildly popular, and considered Israel's greatest king. David was an authentic hero. His accomplishments as a young man were the stuff of legend:

- He was a lowly shepherd boy who became a harp player in Saul's court.

- He slayed the giant Goliath and turned the tide against the Philistines.

- He gallantly participated in battle against the Philistines.

- Like Robin Hood, he led a band of outlaws who robbed the rich in order to share the wealth with the poor.

- He married Michal, the daughter of a king.

- David became king.

King David was also a wise and shrewd politician. Many of his choices reflect great cunning rather than faith, for example, his selection of Michal as his mate. In addition, he killed all of Saul's heirs, preparing the path for his reign. Like so many of the prominent figures of Hebrew Scripture, King David was a remarkable blend of flawed humanity and divine inspiration.

It was David who truly built Israel into a nation. He captured Jerusalem—a real plum for a new king—and changed the name to the City of David—not the most modest move. He also placed the Ark of the Covenant there, symbolizing God's presence in the now holy city. In celebration of the arrival of the Ark, David threw a huge party. It was then that we hear of David dancing naked, which only added to his fame. David also called for a census as a symbol of allegiance to the king.

David also had his fair share of troubles:

- David committed adultery with Bathsheba.

- He arranged the murder of Uriah, Bathsheba's husband.

- He went against God by calling for a census pledging allegiance to the king.

- His son, Absalom, instigated a revolution that almost cost David his crown.

- David was harshly rebuked by the prophet Nathan for having had an affair with Bathsheba.

- Nathan became a real thorn in David's side.

David was a hero all right, but he was also an adulterer, liar, betrayer, and murderer. David was heralded as nearly divine by those who hardly knew him, but as all too human by those who met him face to face.

David's most spiritually significant accomplishment was the celebration of a unique covenant he made with God. This was like no other covenant; it was a covenant between God and king. It surpassed all other covenants in authority, making the king a direct link to God. In a very real sense, the king became the mediator of the will of God. When the king spoke, God spoke.

David not only centralized the government of Israel, he also focused their faith on a relationship between God and their king. It was David who transformed Israel into a true nation. It was David who declared a king to be nearly divine.

Spread the Good Word

Now go and say to my servant David, "This is what the Lord almighty says: I chose you to lead my people Israel when you were just a shepherd boy, tending your sheep out in the pasture. I have been with you wherever you have gone, and I have destroyed all your enemies. Now I will make your name famous throughout the earth! And I have provided a permanent homeland for my people Israel, a secure place where they will never be disturbed. It will be their own land where wicked nations won't oppress them as in the past, from the time I appointed judges to rule my people. And I will keep you safe from all your enemies."

—2 Samuel 7:8–11

Solomon the Splendid

Solomon was the child of David and Bathsheba. He was raised in a king's court by a cunning and conniving mother. His rise to the top was expected. His anointing as king predictable.

Solomon was the wisest of the kings of Israel. He was a true renaissance man. He was a botanist, zoologist, architect, poet, and philosopher. He was also a big spender and loved a lavish lifestyle. He reveled in opulence; no expense was spared in declaring his and Israel's greatness.

Solomon was believed to own 40,000 horses and had 12,000 horsemen just to keep them in shape. He put up a temple in Jerusalem that stood three stories high. It had cedar ceilings and olivewood doors. Absolutely everything was trimmed in gold. The Temple took seven years to build, then Solomon started on a palace for himself and his 700 wives—Solomon liked a lot of everything.

The Bad Word

Enough. That is an important spiritual concept. We live in a culture that does not seem to know the meaning of the word. Neither did Solomon. Solomon paid a huge price for his grandiosity, but it was his own people who were made to pick up the tab.

Solomon's reign lasted 40 years, and during that time, Israel knew peace. He made treaties with Egypt and Tyre. (Tyre was a city in Canaan, next to Sidon in the Gaza strip. It was also once known as Phoenicia.) He maintained a fleet of ships for trade. Solomon built a seaport on the Gulf of Aqabah. He protected his holdings by constructing and maintaining a large fleet of horse-drawn "chariot cities" and other fortifications. He built Israel's wealth by being active in trade and wildly successful in the sale of horses.

Solomon's compulsive building campaign was also the beginning of his downfall. In order to finance it, he taxed his subjects heavily. In order to build it, he used forced labor. The rumblings of discontent exploded in an uprising in the north under the leadership of Jeroboam. Though Solomon was successful in squashing this rebellion, it foreshadowed problems to come.

Solomon had many foreign wives who worshipped many foreign gods, and Solomon went so far as to construct altars to these foreign gods. Now his problems included the wrath of God, who had always been open about being a jealous God.

Solomon was wise in the world's eyes, but not always in the eyes of God. Solomon was too grand and glorious, too willing to stray from his faith to serve himself and his lusts. Solomon simply thought too highly of himself. When Solomon fell, Israel was split by revolution. From this point forward, Israel's history would be an endless string of disasters.

To this very day, these three kings (Saul, David, and Solomon) spiritually and politically dominate the history of Israel.

The Good Word

Solomon is believed to be the author of Proverbs and is known for his wisdom. His judgments in court were praised. In one famous case two women argued over parenthood of a child. Solomon announced that he would split the child in two and each woman would get half. The real mother was horrified and told Solomon to keep the child alive and give her to the other woman. Solomon awarded the child to his real mother—the one who would rather the child live.

It was during their reigns that Israel reached new heights of power and wealth. These were the golden years, a time when God's blessings were many and obvious, an era when God appeared to fulfill his promises to his chosen people. Though there were many moments when the faith of the Hebrews was either tested or glaringly absent, these years when Saul, David, and Solomon ruled were prosperous and peaceful—usually an unbeatable combination.

The Least You Need to Know

- Saul was Israel's first God-appointed king.
- Saul was rejected by the prophet Samuel as well as by the future king David.
- David consolidated power and named Jerusalem after himself.
- David established a special covenant between God and the king.

- Solomon built Israel into a nation of power and peace.
- Solomon constructed a temple and a lavish palace, maintained a fleet of ships and horses, created a booming trade business, and found time for 700 wives and 300 ladies in waiting.

Chapter 7

The Prophets of Israel

In This Chapter

- Upon the death of Solomon in c. 922 A.D., the Kingdom divided
- The Davidic dynasty reigned in Judah, and the Omri dynasty would soon be established in Israel
- The 10 northern tribes revolted against Rehoboam, and Jeroboam became the first king of Israel
- Micaiah, Elijah, and Elisha were the three outstanding prophets of Israel during the Omri dynasty
- The prophets Hosea and Amos predicted doom for Israel

This part of the story begins in 1 Kings 12. We are informed that Rehoboam, the son of Solomon, has been crowned king in Jerusalem. Rehoboam was then sent off to the northern territory to be installed as " king of Israel." In this case, the word *Israel* refers to the 10 northern tribes. Clearly, there was a deep rift between the southern tribes of Judah and the northern tribes of Israel.

Solomon had put the northern tribes into hard labor during his reign, which angered the Israelites, and they demanded that Rehoboam lighten their load. Rehoboam, not possessed of his father's wisdom, told them he intended to only make their work that much harder. That was the straw that broke the camel's back, and all hell broke loose.

Rehoboam sent Adoniram, the taskmaster in charge of forced labor, to try and bring the situation under control. Adoniram was stoned to death. Rehoboam hopped on his chariot and got out of town. The prophet Ahijah predicted that God would tear the 10 tribes of the north away from Solomon.

As you read this chapter, you will begin to see the prominent role played by prophets in the history of Israel. Prophets believed themselves to be messengers from God. Micaiah, Elijah, and Elisha all delivered disturbing messages to Israel. Hosea and Amos went so far as to predict doom for the nation. This chapter will document how prophets sought to expose their people to a truth they did not want to hear.

Jeroboam I

Jeroboam had challenged the authority of Solomon once before, but having been soundly defeated by Solomon, he fled to Egypt. There he was given asylum by the pharaoh Shishak. (1 Kings 11:29–40)

After Solomon's death, Jeroboam returned and was proclaimed king over what was then known as Israel. Jeroboam was an Ephramite, or one from the Northern Kingdom (sometimes referred to as Ephraim, after Jerobam's tribe), so he was not a part of the Davidic dynasty.

While Rehoboam was occupied with the threat of an Egyptian invasion, Jeroboam worked hard at strengthening Israel. He fortified his capital, Shechem. Just as David had tried to unify his kingdom by bringing the Ark to Jerusalem, Jeroboam established two shrines at Dan and Bethel. He also set up a line of priests and called for the celebration of a fall festival, the Feast of Ingathering.

Unfortunately, Jeroboam's reforms went too far. He set up golden bulls in high places other than Jerusalem. It was not Jeroboam's intention to encourage the worship of other gods; he only wished to encourage a renewal of Israel's devotion to the God of the Covenant. The Bull of El, however, was a major god within the Baal religion, and, unwittingly, Jeroboam had linked Israel's faith to that of Canaan.

Historically, Jeroboam became known as the king who taught Israel to sin—not quite the legacy he had hoped for.

The House of Omri

The trouble had started during the reign of Asa of Judah (c. 913–873 B.C.). Asa was interested in religious reform and worked to halt the spread of *syncretism*, the combination of different forms of belief. Asa sought a purified faith, free of foreign influence. During his reign, Israel had grown into a major power. Threatened, Asa took the fateful step of trying to forge an alliance with Syria. Asa's faith and his politics were moving in opposite directions. The Syrian king gladly obliged. Galilee was devastated.

Password

Syncretism is the melting together of different religious customs and beliefs from several different cultures.

Israel would then go through a revolving door of kings. There were assassinations, suicides, and enough intrigue to fill a dozen *James Bond* movies. As often happens, the commander of the army, Omri, rose to power. From a faith standpoint, the Omri dynasty could only be called a bastion of evil. From a political standpoint, the Omri dynasty become one of great power and prestige. Omri was able to initiate a period of collaboration with Judah, which was cemented by a royal marriage between the two houses. Omri was successful against the Moabites and was able to keep the Syrians at bay. He also strengthened his hand by forming an alliance with Phoenicia.

Some geography: The kingdom of Moab lays just above another ancient kingdom, Edom. The river Arnon formed the northern frontier, and the brook Zered shaped the southern frontier. Phoenicia was situated along the Mediterranean Sea, next to Galilee.

The Good Word

Omri was soundly blasted by the Deuteronomic historian. His reign is covered in six verses (1 Kings 16:23–28). In spite of this, history has shown that Omri's reign brought Israel to a time of prosperity and expanded political influence.

Omri built a capital on the hill of Samaria. Samaria was a mighty fortress, strategically positioned to observe any advance from Judah and to gain easy access to Phoenicia. Omri's capital was also to become the home to his luxurious palace. Ahab, Omri's son, continued to build on his father's material progress. But international troubles were on the rise. Assyria would become a major threat, threatening to rule the entire Fertile Crescent.

This threat was so strong that Syria and Israel were forced into alliance—truly strange bedfellows.

The Role of the Prophets

As you can see, the division of the Kingdom combined with syncretism made for a time of spiritual instability. The faith of the Hebrews was constantly being tested or tamed. God was up against a host of fertility gods, and his people were being tempted to pledge allegiance to idols and kings. Into this troubling and unsettling period, several powerful prophets arose.

These prophets played a powerful and prominent role in the religious life of both Israel and Judah:

- Prophets were messengers of God.
- Prophets were sent by God to deliver an often-disturbing message.
- Prophets called upon their people to radically return to their faith.
- Prophets called for a purification of faith, a freeing from foreign influence.
- Prophets told their people not what they wanted to hear, but what they needed to hear.
- Prophets were fearless and spoke boldly to their kings.
- Prophets reminded their people that disobedience would lead to punishment.
- Prophets warned that such punishment might come at the hands of foreign invaders.
- Prophets promised that the road to redemption was paved by obedience.
- Prophets were courageous enough to predict doom.

A Trio of Prophetic Troublers

The story of the prophet Micaiah can be found in 1 Kings 22. Micaiah prophesied during the reign of Ahab in Israel. Ahab wished to go to war against Syria. Jehoshaphat, the king of Judah, agreed to form an alliance with Israel if the prophets agreed. All the prophets concurred with their king, except for one—Micaiah.

Micaiah mocked the other prophets as professional prophets. He stated that the other prophets were mere puppets, paid to agree with their king. Micaiah delivered two oracles. The first predicted that Ahab would be killed. The second made it clear that the Syrian expedition would be a total failure. Micaiah was rebuked and sent to prison. Ahab was killed, and the invasion failed miserably. Micaiah's prophetic word was vindicated.

A Bad Word

True prophets often speak an unpopular brutal truth. Historically, they are frequently met with violent resistance. Prophets are shut up—often in prison.

This was a transitional moment in the history of prophecy. Prophets proclaimed God's judgment *against* the nation and declared a message of doom. Prophecy was no longer linked to nationalism.

Elijah the Tishbite

Israel's history was profoundly impacted by Jezebel. Omri had arranged the marriage of his son Ahab to Jezebel, the daughter of the king of Tyre. Just as Solomon had tried to please his many wives, Ahab wanted to keep Jezebel happy. To do so, he constructed a "temple of Baal," complete with an altar to Asherah, the mother goddess. (1 Kings 16:32–33) Jezebel was a passionate evangelist for her Phoenician religion. This would lead her into direct conflict with the prophets of God, who were just as fanatic in their belief in the covenantal faith of Israel. Jezebel literally tried to rid Israel of every vestige of its traditional faith.

It was during this purge by Jezebel that Elijah appeared on the scene. Elijah's first act was to announce a drought in the name of God. This was a direct challenge to the fertility gods of Baal. (1 Kings 17:1) Elijah went so far as to say that God was in control of fertility in Israel *and* Phoenicia. Elijah was a fierce advocate for the belief that God's claim on his people was total.

Elijah is most famous for his challenge to the 450 prophets of Baal and the 400 of Asherah. Elijah alone represented God and challenged the prophets to end the drought. The ecstatic prophets of Baal performed a rain dance to no avail. Elijah stepped forward to repair an abandoned altar to God and performed a curious ritual of pouring water on wood. The rains came, and the drought was ended. Elijah and God reigned victorious.

Elijah was forced to flee Jezebel, who was out to kill him, and he ran to Judah. Elijah was devastated by the fact that Jezebel remained in power. Where was his God now? On Horeb a divine visitation (an experience of the presence of God) took place, and Elijah's faith was restored. Elijah's return to Sinai symbolized a return to his covenantal faith.

The Good Word

There is another story concerning Elijah: Ahab wanted to purchase the vineyard of Naboth. Naboth believed the land was God's and would not sell. Jezebel, true to form, conspired to have Naboth found guilty of trumped-up charges and had him stoned to death. Elijah confronted Ahab in the vineyard, where Elijah's verbal assault was so strong that Ahab repented. (1 Kings 21:27–29) A king knelt before a prophet, begging to be forgiven. No longer was a king thought of in divine terms.

Elisha the Wonder Full

Though Elisha was Elijah's successor, he was not a prophet like Elijah. The popular lore concerning Elisha was filled with what might be called wonder-tales:

- He parted the Jordan. (2 Kings 2:13–14)
- He purified a spring at Jericho. (2 Kings 2:19–22)
- He multiplied a widow's oil. (2 Kings 4:1–7)
- He raised a dead boy to life. (2 Kings 4:18–37)
- He purified a stew, removing the poison. (2 Kings 4:38–41)

- He healed Naaman of leprosy. (2 Kings 5:1–14)
- He blinded the Aramean army with his prayer. (2 Kings 6:8–23)

These stories were a delight to their listeners, and show us an Elisha who was clearly full of the spirit of God. Most of these stories were set against a backdrop of continued fighting between Syria and Israel.

Amos: The Herdsman from Tekoa

The Southern Kingdom of Judah had a single dynasty from the time of David until its end. The Northern Kingdom had a much more checkered history. The Omri dynasty lasted for the reigns of four kings and was followed by a five-king dynasty, Jehu. The Northern Kingdom remained unstable. The northern tribes believed that God's spirit was poured out on a man, not a dynasty. This thinking led to revolution.

The story of the Jehu dynasty opens in 2 Kings 9. It was Elisha who commissioned Jehu to serve as king. Jehu was a real piece of work, and his reign was brutal:

- He purged Israel.
- He killed Joram, the fugitive king of Israel, and had his body cast into Naboth's vineyard.
- He killed Ahaziah, king of Judah.
- He had Jezebel thrown out a window.
- He had all of Ahab's sons decapitated.

Jehu savagely paved the way for his reign and was soon plagued with problems of his own making. His cold-blooded murder of Ahaziah had alienated the Southern Kingdom, and his extermination of the devotees of the Phoenician Baal had cut off support from Phoenicia. The Syrian king, Hazael, was quick to take advantage of the situation and swept down through the Transjordan. (2 Kings 10:32–33)

Jeroboam II would become the greatest king of the Jehu dynasty. What we know of his reign comes primarily from the books of Amos and Hosea. Without question, this was a time of great prosperity. The marketplaces were jammed, there were luxurious summer and winter homes, and fortresses were mammoth. During Jeroboam II's reign, the commercial activity of the Phoenicians was at its peak.

The Book of Amos addresses the gross economic injustice of this time. Israel shared in the abundant profits gathered from this trade, yet a very oppressive social pyramid had been formed.

A Bad Word

I would contend that too much of today's preaching offers comfort to the already-too-comfortable. I find few preachers with the courage to be prophetic. The primary spiritual issue of our time remains greed and the oppression of the poor. Who have we heard, either religious or political, with the guts to address the gross economic injustice of today's America? Sad!

At the top were the royal courtiers and the merchant class; at the bottom, a mass of impoverished folks. This was a period of economic tyranny, and even the courts were used to support gross injustices.

Amos' prophetic message can be summarized as ...

- A dramatic call for economic, social, and political justice.
- A mocking challenge to the upper class.
- A stern warning that wealth bankrupts faith.
- A strong rebuke for Baal worship.
- A radical call for a return to traditional faith.
- A prediction of doom for Israel.

- An assertion that Israel will be harshly judged by God, because Israel knew God.

- A call for repentance.

Amos bent over backward to counter the false optimism of his time. He strove to jar his people loose, to shake them up and wake them up. He wanted to shatter them out of their comfortable complacency.

Hosea and Gomer

Chaos came after the death of Jeroboam II in 746 B.C. Assyria, under the leadership of Tiglath-pileser III, sought the domination of the Fertile Crescent. Assyria conquered Egypt and Babylonia. Tiglath-pileser III established a military policy of uprooting conquered populations from their homeland and exiling them to remote parts of the Assyrian Empire. Syria and Palestine had good reason to be terrified.

At this time Israel was experiencing a remarkable and tragic level of intrigue. Kings were being knocked off one after another. Hosea's prophetic career overlapped the end of the reign of Jeroboam II and this period of political instability.

Hosea, like Amos, was a prophet of doom. Unlike Amos, however, Hosea offered a ray of hope. He, too, saw a coming Day of Darkness, but he also envisioned a time of restoration and renewal.

The key to understanding Hosea's message is the story of his marriage with Gomer. The highlights of which were ...

- Hosea married Gomer and they had three children.

- Hosea's and Gomer's children were given religious names. Jezreel was a name that commemorated a significant religious site. This would be like having a Christian couple naming their children Bethlehem or Gethsemane.

- Gomer was unfaithful.

- Hosea divorced Gomer.

- Hosea went beyond the law and forgave her.

- Gomer was ransomed and restored as Hosea's wife.

Hosea was the first Israelite prophet to interpret the covenant in terms of marriage. He likened Israel's infidelity to that of his wife, Gomer. Hosea scolded Israel for being unworthy of trust, for breaking the covenant with God. But Hosea also offered Israel a second chance. He offered Israel the same unconditional love, a full restoration of the covenantal relationship, he had granted his wife.

Hosea's personal experience informed and inspired his prophecy. He spoke to Israel with the same anger, hurt, disappointment, and mistrust he knew with Gomer. His rage was equal in magnitude. Yet Gomer was fully restored as his wife, and Hosea's forgiveness was without conditions. Hosea proclaimed that this was the same full restoration of the covenant God offered Israel. Hosea's message was strong and true: Israel would once again be faithful and flourish.

The Least You Need to Know

- The Kingdom divided upon the death of Solomon.
- Judah remained stable under the rule of the Davidic dynasty.
- During the Omri dynasty, prophets addressed the threat of foreign domination and religious influence.
- Micaiah, Elijah, and Elisha challenged the professional court prophets of the king.
- Elijah called upon God to end a drought, soundly defeating the fertility gods of Baal.
- Amos and Hosea predicted doom for Israel; Hosea offered hope of restoration.

Chapter 8

The Prophets of Judah

In This Chapter

- Under the reign of Uzziah, Judah reached the very peak of its economic and military power
- Isaiah's 40-year prophetic career was haunted by the threat of Assyrian invasion and domination
- Micah, like Isaiah, predicted doom for Judah
- Jeremiah, the Weeping Prophet, declared a new personal covenant with God
- Ezekiel, the Priest, was a prophet in exile in Babylon

All the great prophets we have considered up to this point—Elijah, Elisha, Micaiah, Amos, and Hosea—were active in the Northern Kingdom, which parted with the Davidic empire upon Solomon's death. In politics as well as prophesy, the kingdom of Israel overshadowed Judah to the south. Yet Hosea had predicted doom for Israel at the hands of Assyria.

In 721 B.C., Hosea's prophesy came true. After a three-year siege, Samaria fell to the armies of Sargon II. Sargon deported 27,000 Isarelites to Persia and repopulated Israel with colonists from

Babylonia and Syria. Amos' dire prediction, "Fallen is the virgin Israel," had come to pass.

As you read this chapter, you will learn more about the prophets, only this time the context will be Judah. Once again, the great prophets of Judah—Isaiah, Micah, Jeremiah, and Ezekiel—all preach a disturbing message. In spite of the fact that Judah was at the pinnacle of it's political and economic power, the prophets had the audacity to predict doom for their nation. Prophets held their people accountable for their actions. In this chapter, you will see how the prophets of Judah challenge their people to a new relationship with God. Jeremiah will go so far as to call for the establishment of a brand-new covenant.

The Reign of Uzziah

Judah may have lived in Israel's long shadow, but it proved to be the far more stable kingdom. Judah never knew the political chaos and economic discontent that was so much a part of the history of Israel. The dynasty of David remained on the throne the entire time Israel was riddled with political violence and intrigue. Judah also made a smooth transition to the economy of town life and managed to establish a remarkable level of social equality. This stability was also grounded spiritually: Judah believed that God had made a covenant with David, promising to uphold the throne and dynasty.

Under Uzziah, Judah reached the pinnacle of its military and economic power. There is a brief report of this reign in 2 Kings 15:1–7 and a longer version in 2 Chronicles 26. Uzziah's accomplishments were many:

- He modernized the army.
- He gained control of the main commercial highways.
- He expanded commerce into Arabia.
- He reconstructed the seaport of Ezion-geber.
- He led a vigorous development of agriculture.

The only major negative to his reign was in 750 B.C., when Uzziah was stricken with leprosy and confined to a private house.

During this time, Uzziah's son Jotham served as his spokesperson. Though leprosy was widely believed to be a sign of disfavor with God, Uzziah never lost favor with the Judean people. As Israel declined swiftly after the death of Jeroboam II, Judah rose just as quickly. Judah returned to the level of power and influence only known under David and Solomon.

Still, the Assyrian threat loomed on the horizon. Assyria's desire to dominate the Fertile Crescent was well known. With the rise of Tiglath-pileser to power in Assyria, the threat had become a reality.

Isaiah and the Blistered Lips

Isaiah was called to prophesy in the Temple of Solomon. Isaiah's call to prophesy, recorded in Isaiah 6, is one of the most famous passages of all prophetic literature. It is here that we hear of Isaiah having his lips scorched by a red-hot coal (he believed prophets must be purified before they could serve as messengers of God):

> Then one of the seraphim flew over to the altar, and he picked up a burning coal with a pair of tongs. He touched my lips with it and said, "See this coal has touched your lips. Now your guilt is removed, and your sins are forgiven." Then I heard the Lord asking, "Whom should I send as a messenger to my people? Who will go for us?" And I said, "Lord, I'll go! Send me."

—Isaiah 6:6–8

Isaiah was called to be a prophet in this topsy-turvy time. Judah was filled with political and economic hope, yet the Assyrian threat was becoming more ominous by the day. His call is recorded as occurring in 742 B.C.—the same year that Uzziah died and Tiglath-pileser successfully secured Arpad, the capital of a province in northern Syria.

Isaiah's career lasted more than 40 years. During those years, the whole political map of the world changed. Isaiah's prophetic career would know four major political events:

735 B.C.   Syria and Israel invaded Judah and forced Judah to join an alliance against Assyria.

721 B.C.	Shalamaneser V, successor to Tiglath-pileser, laid siege to Samaria, the capital of Israel.
711 B.C.	Sargon II lead the Assyrian army down the Palestine coast to put down another anti-Assyrian revolt.
701 B.C.	Sennacherib lead Assyria's invasion of Judah.

It was against this wild political backdrop that Isaiah's prophetic career took place.

Isaiah was a man of the city and had a deep affection for Jerusalem. He was not greatly affected by either the exodus or the wilderness history. Isaiah was, however, profoundly influenced by the special relationship between God and the Davidic dynasty.

This was Isaiah's prophetic message:

- The Day of God would be one of darkness and judgment.
- Isaiah's earliest message was one of doom.
- Isaiah named his son Shear-yashub (7:3), meaning a remnant shall return to God.
- Isaiah warned that the Israel-Syria-Judah Alliance was a "covenant of death."
- Isaiah affirmed that in times of trouble we must return to faith—absolute trust in God.
- Isaiah told his people to look for a sign.
- The prophet pointed to the birth of a child in the very near future.
- The child would be called Immanuel, meaning "God is with us."
- This wonder child would be of the House of David.
- Isaiah complained of being met by strong resistance. His words fell on deaf ears.
- Isaiah declared Assyria to be the rod of God's anger.
- Isaiah proclaimed that Assyria was destined to rule Judah.
- When the actual invasion came, however, Isaiah made an abrupt about-face and counseled against surrendering to the Assyrian forces.

- Isaiah could not see God destroying Jerusalem or the Davidic dynasty.
- Isaiah saw the building of a new Jerusalem on the foundation of a righteous remnant.

Spread the Good Word

For a child is born to us, a son is given to us. And the government will on his shoulders. These will be his royal titles: Wonderful Counselor, Mighty God, Everlasting Father, Prince of Peace. His ever expanding, peaceful government will never end. He will rule forever with fairness and justice from the throne of his ancestor David. The passionate commitment of the Lord Almighty will guarantee this!

—Isaiah 9:6–8

Much of Isaiah's prophesy became historical fact. Sennacherib suddenly and inexplicably withdrew from Judah, and Jerusalem was spared. Isaiah's strong bond to the Davidic dynasty and covenant remained intact throughout his 40-year career.

The Book of Isaiah contains 66 chapters. Not all the material in those chapters comes from the prophet. A great deal of the book comes from disciples of Isaiah as well as interpreters of the prophet.

Micah, the Rural Prophet

Micah was, in many respects, Isaiah's opposite. He was a prophet who believed that cities were the source of evil. To Micah, cities were bastions of sin and the cause of God's wrath. He also felt no allegiance to the Davidic dynasty and believed God would indeed bring the downfall of Jerusalem. Micah also called upon Israel's sacred history, which is centered in the Exodus, to call his people to return to their faith. The only place where Micah truly sounded like Isaiah was in his predictions of doom.

Micah was a prophet in the spirit of Amos. His message was dominated by the following themes:

- God will judge all false prophets.
- God will judge those nations and leaders who are oppressive of the poor.
- God will not put up with injustice.
- God delights not in sacrifices but justice.
- God promises to provide a new king.

Micah called upon his people to be obedient. He reminded them that true faith led to lives of kindness, compassion, and humility. Micah was a true champion of the poor and a thorn in the side of the wealthy who dwelled in the cities.

Jeremiah and the Tattooed Heart

As is often the case during times of turmoil, Judah began to experience a real nostalgia for the past. Isaiah clearly displayed a longing for the glory days of the reign of David. Judah had long been focused on the Davidic dynasty and covenant. God's special relationship with this dynasty had been Judah's spiritual foundation and the primary source of its great stability.

In the seventh century, Moses and the Mosaic Covenant were rediscovered in Judah. This revival of interest in the Exodus and the wilderness wanderings is recorded in Deuteronomy through 2 Kings. Once again the Exodus would become the fulcrum of the covenantal relationship to God.

During the reign of Ahaz, Judah became no more than a vassal of Assyria. Under Hezekiah, Judah would once again assert its political and religious might. It was during the reign of Mannaseh (687–642 B.C.) that Judah entered its darkest period.

Mannaseh became known as the villain of Judah. He reopened pagan shrines and sacrificed his own son. During this time, many prophets were put to death. Mannaseh ran Judah like a police state. Faith was sacrificed in favor of safety.

When Josiah reigned in Judah and Ashurbanapal—the last great Assyrian king—died in 633 B.C., two prophets burst on the scene. The first was Zephaniah, who preached a message that the Day of God was close at hand. The second was Jeremiah, a prophet strongly influenced by Hosea. Like Zephaniah, Jeremiah was a fierce opponent of syncretism.

Jeremiah was often known as the Weeping Prophet, because his writings were filled with the honest and pain-filled confessions of a man in spiritual torment. Let's briefly review his prophetic career and message:

- He stated that Josiah's reforms fell short because of the shallow repentance of the people.
- He begged the people of Judah to repent.
- He challenged their worship of idols and condemned their selfishness.
- Jerusalem was destroyed because of the sins of the people.
- The people were captured and carried off into Babylonian captivity—this, too, was a result of their disobedience.
- God is the Lord of history.
- God will destroy the nation.
- God will send a new shepherd, a Messiah.
- God will establish a new covenant with his people.
- This covenant will be written upon their hearts.

"The day will come," says the Lord, "when I will make a new covenant with the people of Israel and Judah. This covenant will not be like the one I made with their ancestors when I took them by the hand and brought them out of the land of Egypt. They broke that covenant, though I loved them as a husband loves his wife," says the Lord. "But this is the new covenant that I will make with the people of Israel on that day," says the Lord. "I will put my laws in their minds, and I will write them on their hearts. I will be their God, and they will be my people. And they will not need to teach their neighbors, nor will they need to teach their family, saying, 'You should know the Lord.' For everyone, from the least to the greatest, will already know me," says the Lord. "And I will forgive their wickedness and never again remember their sins." (Jeremiah 31:31–34)

Jeremiah ministered during the reigns of the last five kings of Judah. Jeremiah lived to see many of his prophesies come true, for example, he witnessed the fall of Jerusalem. The key verses to his message are Jeremiah 2:12–13, 3:1–15, and 4:1–4.

It can be fairly said that Jeremiah was the most human of the prophets. By that, I mean that he was certainly the one most willing to reveal his vulnerability and suffering. Much of the Book of Jeremiah could be called confessions.

The Good Word

A change of heart. Jeremiah called upon his people to be converted, to be transformed, to change directions, to be born again. He was asking them to put their whole heart into their faith.

Ezekiel the Priest

Ezekiel was a member of the aristocracy in Jerusalem. He was also in training to be a priest. When King Jehoiachin surrendered, Ezekiel was among the thousands of young men deported from Judah to Babylon. While in exile in Babylonia, he felt called to be a prophet.

Ezekiel was deeply spiritual, and was known to have had many visions. He had a vision that revealed God's moral perfection. He had another vision of the Temple. In this vision, God had cleansed the Temple and restored true worship. The building of a future Temple was shown to Ezekiel in great detail.

Spread the Good Word

On July 31 of my thirtieth year, while I was with the Judean exiles beside the Kebar River in Babylon, the heavens were opened to me, and I saw visions of God. This happened during the fifth year of King Jehoiachin's captivity. The Lord gave a message to me, Ezekiel son of Buzi, a priest, there beside the Kebar River in the land of the Babylonians, and I felt the hand of the Lord take hold of me.

—Ezekiel 1:1–3

Ezekiel also utilized prophetic signs:

- On a clay brick he drew a diagram of Jerusalem under siege. (Ezekiel 4:1–3)
- He laid on his left side for 390 days and on his right for 40 days to indicate the number of years that Israel and Judah would be punished respectively. (Ezekiel 4:4–8)
- He cut off his hair with a sword and separated it into three parts, portraying the fate of Jerusalem. (Ezekiel 5:1–12)
- He packed his bags and dug through a wall to show how people would have to flee. (Ezekiel 12:1–16)
- He ate and drank while trembling madly to show the fear people would know in the coming siege. (Ezekiel 12:17–20)

Ezekiel could be called eccentric, even mad, but I believe he was willing to use any means necessary to grab the attention of his people. I think Ezekiel was dramatic and willing to use the skills of living theater to get his message across.

Ezekiel's message was dramatically influenced by Jeremiah:

- Ezekiel addressed his people as a covenant community—"the house of Israel."

- Israel had always been a morally corrupt nation.

- Israel had spiritually compromised too often.

- The fall of Jerusalem and the Babylonian exile were the result of disobedience—both were divinely ordained.

- The nation as well as the individual was responsible for their sin.

- The distance between a pure and holy God and human sinners was enormous.

- The unfaithful priests and clergy were condemned as shepherds who led their flocks astray.

- The perfect shepherd, the Messiah, would come and serve as a faithful watchman.

- The Temple would be cleansed by God, and true worship would be restored.

- Ezekiel maintained his priestly tradition by returning the Temple to the center of faith.

- He envisioned the restoration of a united Judah and Israel.

Up until the fall of Jerusalem in 586 B.C., Ezekiel's message was wholly one of doom. After the fall, the message was transformed into one of hope. Israel was promised restoration. God's punishment was complete. The captivity had deepened and strengthened the faith of the exiles.

The messages of the prophets were raw and radical. They called for a radical return to a traditional faith and claimed that God would reward faithfulness and punish disobedience. The nation's history was in the hands of a just God. The fall of a nation was the result of being a sinful society. Restoration was the result of a transformed faith. The prophets were fearless in predicting doom and just as courageous in announcing hope.

Prophets spoke from and to the heart. Their words were often scathing and brutal. Prophets sought to pierce the calluses that were covering true faith. They attacked the sinful ways of the world and called their people to higher ground. They not only met stiff resistance to their message, but they also often lost their lives. The world had little use for those who dared call humanity to lives of equality and justice for all.

The Least You Need to Know

- Isaiah warned that an alliance with Syria and Israel was a covenant with death for Judah.

- Isaiah predicted doom at the hands of Assyria.

- Isaiah promised the coming of a sign—a child called Immanuel.

- Micah predicted doom and demanded justice.

- Jeremiah declared a new covenant, one written on the heart.

- Ezekiel prophesied while in exile in Babylon and promised the coming of the Good Shepherd.

Chapter 9

The Poets

In This Chapter

- The Psalter gives an overview of Israel's history
- Wisdom literature strives to find the meaning of life
- Wisdom is always a divine gift
- Wisdom is often rooted in despair
- Song of Solomon is one lusty book

There is a whole section of the Hebrew Scripture that has nothing to do with the Day of God, the covenant, the Law, the prophesy, or any Messianic hope. It is writing rooted in day-to-day life. It is writing from the heart. It is the voice of the poets.

Without question, a bulk of Hebrew Scripture is devoted to the activity of God in the history of Israel as a people and as a nation. Although the poets still address the activity of God, they move on a much more personal level, and their focus is on how God speaks to the spiritual longings of the individual.

Poets speak to the meaning of life. It is their calling to express the yearnings of human beings. They raise life's most difficult questions and speak to and about the soul in despair or distress. Above all else, the poets ponder the mysteries of life. They seek not to unravel the mysteries, but to point to those mysteries as a revelation of the transcendence of God.

As you read this chapter, you will become better acquainted with the Psalter (all 150 Psalms) and the wisdom literature (Proverbs, Ecclesiastes, and Job) of Hebrew Scripture. It is here that you will discover the true intimacy the Hebrew people felt with and for their God. Even sex is shared with God, as you will see in the Song of Solomon. God is a friend with whom you can share anything—anger, fear, doubts, disappointment, joy, hopes, and dreams. The Hebrew people brought everything to their God.

The Psalter

The Book of Psalms is, in many respects, an overview of the history of Israel. The Psalter clearly establishes Israel as a worshipping community. As you read the Psalms, you are experiencing the deep and powerful faith of a people in prayer and praise.

The Psalter is modeled after the Torah and divided into an introduction and five distinct books:

- Introduction—Psalm 1
- Book I—Psalms 2–41
- Book II—Psalms 42–72
- Book III—Psalms 73–89
- Book IV—Psalms 90–106
- Book V—Psalms 107–156

The relationship of King David to the Psalter is like that of Moses to the Torah. He is the author, the model, and the source of inspiration. David is the heart of the Psalter.

There are three forms of psalms:

- **Hymns.** Psalms that sing the praise of God.
- **Laments.** Psalms that expose problems and speak eloquently of God's absence.
- **Thanksgiving.** Psalms that are a curious combination of both hymns and laments. Gratitude is often discovered in grief.

There were also the Zion Psalms (46, 48, 76, 84, 87, and 122), which declare that God resided in Zion or Jerusalem, and the Royal Psalms (2, 20, 21, 45, 72, and 110), which are prayers on behalf of the king. As you can see, the Psalms clearly reflect a devotion to the Davidic covenant.

The Good Word

An excellent example of a hymn of praise is Psalm 100. Psalm 22 is a good example of a personal lament. Psalms 10, 74, 79, 106, and 137 are community-based laments. Psalm 51 is a model for a penitential psalm.

One of the great beauties of the Psalms is the intimacy with God they express. God is spoken to as a friend, a counselor, and at times, even an enemy. The Psalms express everything from rage to praise, worry to wonder, sorrow to joy.

Some Psalms are rooted in deep despair. Some are shouted from the tops of spiritual peaks. These people of faith felt comfortable sharing everything with their God—no holds barred.

The following are two examples from the Psalms:

> Shout with joy to the Lord, O Earth!
> Worship the Lord with gladness.
> Come before him, singing with joy,
> Acknowledge that the Lord is God!
> He made us, and we are his.
> We are his people, the sheep of his pasture.
> Enter his gates with thanksgiving;
> go into his courts with praise.
> Give thanks to him and bless his name.
> For the Lord is good.
> His unfailing love continues forever,
> and his faithfulness continues to each generation.

—Psalm 100

My God, my God! Why have you forsaken me?
Why do you remain so distant?
Why do you ignore my cries for help?
Every day I call to you, my God, but you do not answer.
Every night you hear my voice, but I find no relief.

—Psalm 22:1–2

The Wisdom Literature

Wisdom comes from God. We can only receive it. God inspires it.
God infuses us with it. God informs our hearts, takes the scales
from our eyes, and unplugs our ears. The fog lifts, and we can finally see. The curtain goes up, and the play comes to life. The light
goes on, and things make sense.

Wisdom is grounded in pain. It is fueled by suffering and sorrow.
Many times we must be on our knees long enough to know that we
are not God. We have to hit bottom before we can look up. We
have to let go—to lose control—before we can let God in.

Wisdom is surrender. It is waving the white flag. It is knowing that
God alone is in charge. God controls history. God is transcendent
and mysterious. God is also close and intimate. God is a fusion of
opposites: divine and human, easy to find and impossible to locate,
present and absent.

Wisdom is revelation. It is God coming to us. It is a glimpse of
grace, a glimpse of heaven. It is eternity in our midst. Wisdom is
when God speaks and humans listen, when God points the way and
humans follow, when God instructs and humans learn.

Wisdom literature is a quest to address the meaning of life. Much of
it is attributed to Solomon, under whose reign many foreign cultures flourished. Wisdom literature clearly shows evidence of this
foreign influence. Solomon was claimed as a source of wisdom in
1 Kings 3:28 and 1 Kings 4:33. Wisdom literature seeks to offer insight and advice to the young as well as reflection and renewal to
the mature.

Ecclesiastes

I love Ecclesiastes and preach from it on a regular basis. I appreciate its humanity, cherish the fact that it embraces human despair, and treasure its rigorous honesty. Ecclesiastes is attributed to Solomon. It speaks of how meaningless, predictable, and routine life can become, of how life can become a rut.

Solomon cautions that the only difference between a rut and a grave is the depth. He warns of the petty complaints and concerns of life and asks us to leave the petty life behind. Ultimately, Ecclesiastes speaks to the emptiness of life.

Solomon acknowledges the pain that comes from feeling everything is futile. He also asserts that God alone can fill the empty space inside us. Only God can provide the meaning and worth we seek. What we seek is grace—unconditional love. God is that grace.

A Bad Word

Many folks see faith as the elimination of despair. That is unwise. Faith is the embracing of despair and squeezing out the hope! Faith without the experience of despair is shallow faith, the trivial pursuit of good feelings, not the true source of a good life.

Proverbs

A proverb is a snippet of wisdom. Solomon's Proverbs are divided into three categories:

- Wisdom for young people (1:1–9:18)
- Wisdom for all people (10:1–24:34)
- Wisdom for leaders (25:1–31:31)

Many of the proverbs address ordinary problems such as laziness (6:6–11) or drunkenness (23:20–21). Many give advice on building loving and loyal relationships; strong friendships and family are a consistent focus of Proverbs.

The Proverbs also address the importance of our speech—being true to our word; our work—to be carried out with discipline and devotion; our success—the result of strong character and personal integrity, not worldly fame or fortune.

Solomon thought of people in two ways: the wise, who are willing to see their lives through God's eyes and are ready to obey, and fools, who choose to ignore God on a daily basis. Solomon believed we have a choice between a petty life of fleeting pleasure and a deeply faithful life of eternal satisfaction.

For example …

> By wisdom the Lord founded the earth; by understanding he established the heavens. By his knowledge the deep fountains of the earth burst forth, and the cloud poured down rain. My child, don't lose sight of good planning and insight. Hang on to them, for they fill you with life and bring you honor and respect. They keep you safe on your way and keep your feet from stumbling. You can lie down without fear and enjoy pleasant dreams. You need not be afraid of disaster or the destruction that comes upon the wicked, for the Lord is your security. He will keep your foot from being caught in a trap.
>
> —Proverbs 3:19–26

Essentially, Solomon's proverbs form an anthology. They are the rich legacy of wisdom he wanted to leave his children, his grandchildren, and his nation. The Proverbs are a gathering of his insights, observations, reflections, revelations, and glimpses into his own heart and the heart of God.

Every one of us is called upon to leave behind a collection of proverbs. We are each meant to take our lives just that seriously. We are each intended to live in such a way that we make an imprint on the human heart. We leave behind those insights and beliefs that we felt mattered; found too good not to be true; and gave our lives a sense of purpose, a value, a meaning. What proverbs could you write today? Do it!

Job

Job is everyone. Job is a study of the human relationship to God. Job is not a story of a man drowning in tragedy, it is the tale of one man's triumph of faith. It is a book that addresses why good people suffer.

Job had lost his possessions, his children, and his health. He struggled with why, in spite of his righteous life, he suffered so. He shared this pain with his friends, and his friends responded with callus assertions that he must have done something wrong he couldn't remember doing or that only God knew about. Job's friends clung to the dogma and doctrine of blessings and curses: If you are suffering, you are being punished; if you are being punished, you somehow disobeyed!

Job was counseled by a young man, Elihu, who said that his friends were wrong and that he was being punished to correct his arrogance. Job's suffering was being used by God to make him humble. God himself finally answered Job. His answer sounded mighty harsh: He basically told Job he had no right to question God's actions. I suspect that what is truly meant here is that the mystery of God must be lifted up and declared. Life does not always offer answers. At times, all life can offer is an occasion for faith.

Job was forced to accept that even in suffering, God must be enough. He was challenged to believe even in the absence of an answer. This was the true test of faith: to believe when everything and everyone tells you not to. Faith, at times, cannot point to the answer. At times, all faith can do is point to the mystery.

> Then the Lord asked Satan, "Have you noticed my servant Job? He is the finest man in all the earth—a man of complete integrity. He fears God and will have nothing to do with evil. And he has maintained his integrity, even though you persuaded me to harm him without cause."
>
> —Job 2:3

There are many aspects of Job that pose real problems for me. I have a tough time accepting the notion of God being influenced by Satan. I struggle with the idea of God being willing to inflict needless suffering on anyone. To be honest, I even find God's assertion that Job has no right to question God's ways more than a bit inadequate.

The book of Job can be broken down as follows:

- Job is tested. (1:1–2:13)

- Job gets poor answers from his friends. (3:1–31:40)

- A young man tries to offer Job a reasonable explanation. (32:1–37:24)

- God offers a tough answer. (38:1–41:34)

- Job experiences a restoration of faith. (42:1–17)

The book of Job offers the poignant story of one man's spiritual journey. It is not a picnic or a vacation. It is a long walk down a difficult path.

The Song of Solomon

I don't exactly know where to place The Song of Solomon. It is definitely poetry, although it is definitely not a Psalm. I have a hard time thinking of it as *wisdom literature*.

Make no mistake about it, The Song of Solomon is one erotic piece of writing. If you have ever wondered what the difference is between pornography and erotic literature, read The Song of Solomon. There is nothing pornographic about Solomon's explicit testament to the joys of sex.

The Song of Solomon is a celebration of the joys and beauty of sex and sexuality. It is a magnificent declaration of how the fusion of a man and a woman becomes a true expression of the love of God. Since Solomon had more than his fair share of wives and lovers, he must have considered himself an expert on the subject. I am shocked that he showed as much insight on the subject as he did.

Though it can be said that this brief book also affirms the marriage between God and his people, its primary message is simply to share the beauty and joy of making love. It does, however, declare the importance of commitment as the foundation upon which sex should be experienced. It also speaks to the vital importance of loyalty in a marriage and the reality that every marriage will know times of conflict and the need for reconciliation.

A Bad Word

Religion is notorious for being uncomfortable with the subject of sex. This is a shame, because sex is a gift from God. Too often I hear adults speak only of the dangers and abuses of sex, seldom commenting on the joys and pleasures. Solomon was remarkably at ease with the subject. His writing is poetic and profound; he truly celebrates sex as a gift; he offers a portrait of marriage as a home to pleasure.

The Least You Need to Know

- The Psalms of David provide insight into Israel's history.
- The Psalms record an intimate relationship with God.
- Ecclesiastes embraces his despair with arms of faith.
- Proverbs offers advice on meaningful living.
- Job embraced his suffering as a condition of being human.
- The Song of Solomon celebrates sex and marriage.

Part 4

Christian Scripture: Jesus' Beginnings

We turn now to the Christian Scripture. As you might imagine, the Christian Scripture is focused on the life, message, and ministry of Jesus. We see Jesus as preacher and teacher—a rabbi. We hear of Jesus the healer and miracle-maker. Christian Scripture also deals with the actions of his disciples and followers, the difficult formation of the early church, and the struggles of humanity with the enormous uncertainty of their future.

Christian Scripture is a tragic and triumphant saga. It is the tale of a most ordinary man who sought to transform the world by way of an extraordinary faith, hope, and love. It is about the world who hated him; the family who could not understand him; the friends who loved, denied, doubted, and betrayed him; the hometown that rejected him; and the many outcasts, losers, and nobodies who claimed him to be the Christ.

The bond between the Hebrew and Christian Scripture is tightly woven. It is fair to say that without understanding Jesus as a Jew, well versed in the Torah, we cannot possibly comprehend the impact of Jesus' prophetic teaching and preaching; the irony of who he chose to be his disciples, and who chose him to be their Lord; or the offensiveness of the claims to be the Messiah.

Chapter 10

In the Beginning— the Sequel

In This Chapter

- The birth of Jesus fulfilled prophesy
- Luke tells the traditional Christmas story
- Matthew tells of Herod and the three wise men
- Much of Jesus' childhood and adolescence is left untold
- John the Baptist paves the way for the ministry of Jesus

Have you ever told a story? Of course you have. We all have. Being a good storyteller, however, takes a lot of practice. It is an art, a skill, a calling.

The key to being a good storyteller is to capture the audience from the very beginning, just as a good book grabs the reader from the first page. A good story requires a great beginning.

The story of Jesus is often called "the greatest story ever told." That is a matter of opinion and faith. It definitely is a good story. It was a story first shared orally, and since it spread like wildfire, we can assume that it was transmitted by some fine storytellers.

As the story evolved, written down in the language of faith, the tale began to weave a web of gospel truth. It told a story that appealed to everyone, had meaning everywhere, and conveyed a message suited for all time. It became a story that was magical, mysterious, even miraculous. The beginnings of this story were all three.

As you read this chapter, you will learn of the humble beginnings of Jesus' life and ministry. His was not a royal birth; Jesus was born a commoner. This ordinary story will quickly turn extraordinary, heralded by the arrival of three wise men from the east. This chapter will also highlight what little we know about Jesus' childhood and adolescence.

Jesus' Life

The beginnings of Jesus' life, as recorded in Christian Scripture, accomplished the following:

- Declared that the life of Jesus Christ was a historical point of demarcation—time was split in two.

- Announced that Jesus brought a whole new way of life to the world; the values of the world were turned upside down.

- Asserted that the whole Creation was transformed by a child born in Bethlehem.

From the very beginning, Christian Scripture lets us know that nothing will ever be the same again. Jesus ushered in a new age. Still, the truth of Christian Scripture remains a matter of belief—a leap of faith.

Prophesy Fulfilled

Prophets saw themselves as messengers sent by God. The message they delivered often contained signs. These signs pointed to a coming event of great consequence. Prophetic signs served to foreshadow the future.

Many Christians hold that the birth of Jesus was predicted by the prophets of Hebrew Scripture. This interpretation contends that in Jesus Christ we see the fulfillment of prophesy—that event to which the signs point has arrived. Whether or not you agree with this interpretation of Scripture depends on your faith perspective. The story of Jesus' birth and the events that surround it, do, however, conform closely to many of the prophetic images found in Hebrew Scripture.

O Come, O Come, Immanuel (Isaiah 7:10–17)

> Look! The virgin will conceive a child! She will give birth to a son and will call him Immanuel—"God is with us."
>
> —Isaiah 7:14

The Gospel of Matthew quotes Isaiah 7:14 as prophesy fulfilled with the birth of Jesus. (Matthew 1:18–25) A young woman or virgin is to give birth to a son named Immanuel. By naming her son Immanuel, the young woman displayed her complete trust in God. The fact that the child would eat cream and honey indicated that this would be a time of plenty for those who survived the devastation predicted for Syria, Israel, and Judah.

The Messianic King (Isaiah 9:1–7)

> For a child is born to us, a son is given to us. And the government will rest upon his shoulders. These will be his royal titles: Wonderful Counselor, Mighty God, Everlasting Father, Prince of Peace.
>
> —Isaiah 9:6

The child would be the Messiah. Christian Scripture and faith hold that Jesus is the long-awaited Messiah. Matthew quoted these verses in describing the ministry of Jesus. (Matthew 4:15–16) The northern territories of Zebulun and Naphtali are where Jesus grew up and frequently ministered.

Jesus called himself "the light of the world." (John 8:12) Christian Scripture holds that Jesus will deliver us from darkness and slavery

to sin; that he will establish an eternal Kingdom over which he will
govern; and that he is, in fact, the Prince of Peace.

The Servant Songs (Isaiah 42:1–4, 49:1–6, 50:4–9, 52:13–53:12)

> But he was wounded and crushed for our sins. He was beaten
> that we might have peace. He was whipped, and we were
> healed!
>
> —Isaiah 53:5

Christian Scripture contends that Jesus is the suffering servant depicted in the prophesy of Isaiah. Jesus is the man despised and rejected. Jesus is the man well-acquainted with grief. Jesus is the man
whose life is a living sacrifice for others. Jesus is the sacrificial lamb.
Jesus is the one punished for the world's sins.

The Good Shepherd (Ezekiel 34:1–31)

> For this is what the Sovereign Lord says: I myself will search
> and find my sheep. I will be like a shepherd looking for his
> scattered flock. I will find my sheep and rescue them from all
> places to which they were scattered on that dark and cloudy
> day.
>
> I will bring them back home to their own land of Israel from
> among the peoples and nations.
>
> —Ezekiel 34:11–13

Here the duties of a real shepherd are applied to the rulers of the
people of Israel. Christian Scripture often refers to Jesus as the
Good Shepherd, the one who truly cares for his flock. Jesus rescues
the lost sheep. He guards his sheep against danger. He holds his
flock together as one. He leads his flock to greener pastures.

An Answer for Job (Job 38:1–41:34)

> Who is this that questions my wisdom with such ignorant
> words?
>
> —Job 38:2

When Job asked why he suffered so, God's final answer was to tell Job he had no right to question God.

Jesus became God's answer for Job. Why did Job suffer? Because even God's own son suffered!

Something New Under the Sun (Ecclesiastes 1:1–18)

> "Everything is meaningless," says the Teacher, "utterly meaningless!"
>
> —Ecclesiastes 1:2

The Book of Ecclesiastes declares a preacher's despair. It asks life's most basic and disturbing question: "What is the point?"

The despair described is the result of the circular nature of life. Everything we experience is predictable, even boring. There is nothing new under the sun. Everything is the same old thing. Round and round we go, and where we stop nobody knows—or cares.

Christian Scripture asserts that Jesus is something new under the sun. Jesus makes everything brand new. Jesus transforms all of creation into new life.

The Traditional Christmas Story (Luke 2:1–20)

> And while they were there, the time came for her baby to be born. She gave birth to her first child, a son. She wrapped him snugly in strips of cloth and laid him in a manger, because there was no room for them in the village inn.
>
> —Luke 2:6–7

One story often read on Christmas Eve is the account of Jesus' birth from the Gospel of Luke. This version is found only in Luke. John and Mark do not record the miraculous events surrounding the birth of Jesus, and Matthew tells the story from another angle.

The story, as recorded in Luke, offers a depiction not only of the birth of Jesus but also a perspective on his ministry and message as well:

- Jesus was born in Bethlehem, as Micah had predicted. (Micah 5:2)

- Mary and Joseph could not find a place to stay—there was once again no room for Jesus.

- Jesus' was a most lowly birth. He was literally born in a barn out back, an outcast.

- Jesus' parents were folks of no power, prestige, or possessions.

- Mary and Joseph were of the house of David, and so maintained the royal line prophesied in Hosea 3:5.

- Shepherds rushed to see the babe in Bethlehem.

- Shepherds were scorned by the religious elite, as their work kept them from performing the ceremonial washings necessary for service in the Temple.

The Good Word

Jesus was born in a fashion opposite of what the world expected for the birth of a king. The world looked for signs of wealth and power. Jesus' birth was one of poverty and powerlessness. The world looked for the birth of the Messiah to capture the whole world's attention. The birth of Jesus only drew a response from lowly shepherds. The world wanted a great military champion as the Messiah, one who would vanquish all foes. Jesus came as a Messiah who was the champion of the poor and outcast, one who arrived to vanquish sin and death. Jesus turned the world's values upside down. Jesus was neither what the world expected, nor what it wanted. God seldom gives the world what it wants, but rather what it needs. The world needed Jesus.

Luke set the stage for Jesus to be the true champion of the poor. Jesus served those in need. He elevated those of low degree, those at the bottom of the barrel. His was a ministry grounded not in greatness by the world's standards, but on grace, the only standard of God. From this lowly birth, a nobody born to a nobody, came a deep love and respect for all of the world's nobodies.

In Jesus, everyone becomes a somebody ... somebody special ... someone worthy of respect.

Spread the Good Word

The gifts that were brought by the magi can also be seen as having symbolic meaning:

- **Gold.** Commonly given to kings. Jesus is thought of as king.

- **Frankincense.** A gift given to priests. It is the sweet perfume used in Temple services. Jesus is thought of as High Priest.

- **Myrrh.** A gift given to someone about to die. It is used in embalming. This gift may foreshadow Jesus' ultimate fate.

Herod and the Astrologers (Matthew 2:1–12)

The Gospel of Matthew offers a birth story from a whole new viewpoint. Both stories are independent. As an editor, Matthew was interested in presenting clear and compelling evidence that Jesus was the Messiah, especially to the Jews. Matthew told the birth story, then, including material he believed would have special appeal to the Jews:

- This birth story highlighted Herod.

- Herod was in favor with many Jews because he orchestrated a major renovation of the Temple.

- Herod's third wife, Mariamne, was of Jewish royalty.

- Herod was not the rightful heir to the throne of David, and so if Jesus was a true heir, this meant major trouble.

- The three kings were, in fact, Persian holy men—magi.

- Magi were known for great wisdom and skill in the areas of medicine, natural science, and philosophy.

- Magi were also skilled interpreters of dreams and gifted astrologers.

- Since the Jews were held in Babylonian captivity, they were aware of magi.

- The star the magi followed signals God's direct involvement in the life of Israel.

The Good Word

The debates about the wise men have been waged for centuries. Were there three or two? Were they kings or astrologers? Where in the east were they from? There appears to be no conclusive evidence.

What we do know is that the arrival of foreigners, wealthy enough to bring lavish gifts, had great symbolic meaning. It tells us that Jesus was to be Savior to all. It speaks to the fact that the wisdom of the world must bow before the wisdom of God.

Matthew's version of the birth of Jesus can be seen as a direct challenge to the Jews. By having foreigners traveling thousands of miles to worship Jesus, Matthew made it clear that this Messiah was king of the world, not just Judea.

The story of the wise men continues to fascinate. Three men took a huge risk in following a star. Three wise adults knelt before a babe. Three kings worshipped a rag-wrapped child in a barn. The images are indeed striking. The message is powerful.

The Wonder Years

In many respects, we know little to nothing of Jesus' childhood and adolescence. We do have a few Biblical references to this period of his life, and we can make some educated deductions.

All of our assumptions are based on who Jesus became as an adult. It is unlikely that Jesus became the man he did, with the values and ethics he held dear, without having been strongly influenced by his family, friends, and community during his formative years.

Here is a survey of some of what the Bible tells us about Jesus' growing-up, as well as some thoughtful speculations:

- Jesus came from a middle-class family.
- Jesus' family was devoutly Jewish.
- In accordance with Jewish law, Jesus was circumcised eight days following his birth. (Luke 2:21)
- Mary came with an offering of two pigeons to mark her purification after childbirth. Again, this rite of purification was in keeping with Jewish law. (Luke 2:22–24)
- For the sum of five shekels, Mary and Joseph bought back their child from God. This, too, was in strict adherence to Jewish ceremonial law. (Luke 2:27)
- Jesus was recognized as the Messiah by Simeon (Luke 2:25–32) and Anna (Luke 2:36–38). Both Simeon and Anna were known to be extremely devout.
- Jesus came from a home comfortable with prayer.
- Jesus came from a home remarkably comfortable with women.
- Jesus was well versed in Hebrew Scripture.
- Jesus was powerfully influenced by the Pharisees.
- Jesus was powerfully influenced by the Hebrew prophets.
- Jesus attended his first Passover in Jerusalem at age 12.

- Jesus was recognized for being wise beyond his years. (Luke 2:41–50)

- Jesus was trained to be compassionate to those in need or to those who suffer.

- Jesus remained celibate.

- Joseph died before Jesus began his ministry. Mary was at the Wedding in Cana, but no mention is made of Joseph.

Over the course of Jesus' childhood and adolescence, he clearly began to discern a calling for himself. It was slowly revealed to him that he was meant to fulfill a unique task. His heart informed him of the need to embark upon a perilous spiritual journey. His longings tugged him down a road less traveled.

Spread the Good Word

When Jesus' parents had fulfilled all the requirements of the law of the Lord, they returned home to Nazareth in Galilee. There he grew up healthy and strong. He was filled with wisdom beyond his years, and God placed his special favor upon him.

—Luke 2:39–40

Rebel with a Cause

Jesus was no ordinary, devout Jewish youth. Early on he began to question the integrity of the religious elite—the Pharisees. He saw them as hypocrites, phonies, people who talk a good line but don't live it. Jesus was offended by their lack of compassion for the poor and their lack of love for those rejected by the world. Jesus' willingness to sit down and discuss matters of the Law with his elders showed he was unusually confident of his convictions.

I suspect that as a teen Jesus was already showing signs of being rebellious—not in the sense of acting out or up, but in challenging authority. Jesus was to become a man who incessantly challenged authority. Jesus was a revolutionary. The seeds of his longing to turn the world upside down and inside out were planted at a young age.

In Jesus, these seeds grew into a strong and fearless faith. Jesus became a fierce advocate for spiritual and ethical revolution. He challenged the religious elite to preach good news to the poor and to release all captives. He chided the political powers of his time with a call for justice and equality. Jesus was no sweet, young lad. He was a young man with a burning desire to build the Kingdom of God on this earth.

The Good Word

Jesus was a nonconformist. He rejected the idea of conforming to the standards and values of the world. He chose instead to conform only to what he believed God would want.

The Least You Need to Know

- Christian Scripture claims that Jesus is the Messiah, the fulfillment of Hebrew prophesy.

- The Gospel of Luke offers a birth story that establishes a deep connection between Jesus and the poor and the needy.

- The Gospel of Matthew makes an effort to tell of Jesus' birth in a manner appealing to the Jews.

- Mary and Joseph observed all the appropriate Jewish ceremonies for a newborn.

- Jesus was well versed in Hebrew Scripture but grew increasingly upset with the hierocracy of the Pharisees.

- Jesus displayed the powerful influence of the Hebrew prophets on his heart and mind: He was a champion of the poor, unafraid to challenge religious or political authority, and called for a new world order.

11

Jesus and the Disciples

In This Chapter

- The spiritual life is never solo
- Jesus chose 12 disciples
- Jesus celebrated diversity in making his choices
- Disciples were called to a life of discipline
- The central task of discipleship is mercy

The spiritual life is never lived in isolation. Jesus came to this earth as the ideal role model for the spiritual life. One of the major lessons he taught was not to try and go it alone. The spiritual life requires support. Community is the place where the Holy Spirit dwells. Faith thrives within a spiritual family. Jesus was aware of the vital importance of sharing ministry.

He was conscious that his ministry would be difficult. There would be sorrow and suffering, and there would be ample pain and even persecution. Jesus was convinced of the importance of sharing these struggles with trusted friends.

Jesus also believed in empowering people. He challenged his disciples to use their gifts. He called them to be ministers. He enabled them to become bearers of good news. Jesus freed those 12 men to become the individuals they were meant to be: loving, kind, compassionate, capable of healing, and courageous enough to build the Kingdom.

As you read this chapter, you will become aware of the extraordinary diversity of Jesus' chosen disciples. You will learn a bit of background on each of the 12, as well as some of what Jesus expected from them. This chapter will reveal Christ's call to be merciful—the essence of discipleship. Discipleship is to *be* an instrument of God's grace.

Who Were the Twelve?

We know little of the disciples. The Biblical references are few, and we get only a glance or a glimpse of their character. Here is a thumbnail sketch of the Jesus' 12 disciples (in no particular order):

- **Simon Peter.** A fisherman. Peter was called "the rock"—the foundation for the future church. Peter was also called Satan when he urged Jesus to reject the cross. He denied knowing Jesus during the time of the crucifixion. He became the fiery preacher of Pentecost and, along with Paul, a prominent leader of the early church.

- **James (Son of Zebedee).** A fisherman. Along with his brother John, he asked for a special place of honor in the Kingdom. He also asked to have a Samaritan village destroyed. He and his brother John were called "Sons of Thunder." He was ambitious and short-tempered. He died a martyr.

- **John (Son of Zebedee).** A fisherman. The other "Sons of Thunder," he cared for Jesus' mother after Jesus' death. A beloved and trusted friend to Jesus. He became a leader in the Jerusalem church.

- **Andrew.** A fisherman. Brother of Peter. Accepted John the Baptist's testimony about Jesus. Evangelical—wanted to bring others to believe in Jesus.

- **Philip.** A fisherman. Questioned how Jesus could feed 5,000. He asked Jesus to show him God the Father. He had a questioning and probing mind.

- **Bartholomew (Nathanael).** He initially rejected Jesus for having come from Nazareth. He was later acknowledged by Jesus for his honesty, and he acknowledged Jesus as "King of Israel" when they met. He was called a "true son of Israel."

- **Matthew (Levi).** A tax collector. Tax collectors were despised, and he was a social outcast due to his job. He invited Jesus to a party with his buddies. Many feel he wrote the Gospel of the same name.

- **Thomas (the Twin).** A man of great faith. He told the disciples to accompany Jesus to Bethany, even at the risk of death. A man of great doubt, Thomas refused to believe in the risen Christ until he could touch his wounds.

- **James (Son of Alphaeus).** Often known as James the Less. Less is right—we know zip about him.

- **Thaddeus (Judas, Son of James).** He wanted Jesus to reveal himself to the world, not just to his followers.

- **Simon the Zealot.** We only know what his name implied— he was a fierce patriot.

- **Judas Iscariot.** A deeply devoted disciple, he sank into despair as he realized the ministry was drawing to a close. Felt betrayed by Jesus' seeming acceptance of the cross. Betrayed Jesus. Killed himself.

These 12 were to be Jesus' spiritual family and personal friends. They were chosen to share the myriad tasks of ministry. They were selected to be the first work force to try and build the Kingdom.

Why These Guys?

It is hard to discern why Jesus chose these particular 12. We haven't a clue as to how he made his choices. What was it he saw in these men? Did he just know? Did he take a huge risk and select randomly? Was there some kind of spiritual connection he experienced or felt?

I don't really know, but I suspect the following factors motivated Jesus' choices:

- He wanted ordinary men with ordinary jobs. Since he intended to preach and teach to ordinary folks, Jesus wanted disciples with whom these folks could easily identify.

- He wanted diversity, so he chose men of remarkably different backgrounds and temperaments. Diversity is the hallmark of Creation and also critical to creativity.

- Jesus did not want 12 clones of himself—no sparks, no spiritual fires.

- Jesus wanted disciples who were human.

- He did not want religious fanatics or folks who lived lives separate from the real world.

- He wanted individuals who were willing to question and doubt. He did not want blind obedience or faith.

- Jesus wanted friends. He chose men with whom he felt comfortable.

- Jesus wanted leaders, at least individuals he hoped would carry on his ministry after he was gone.

The Good Word

I love the humanness of these disciples. They argued with Jesus. They got jealous over favored treatment. They questioned his wisdom. They doubted his divinity. They betrayed him. Even Peter, the one who he said he would build his church upon, managed to claim three times that he did not even know Jesus. And this came at the time when Jesus needed him most. The disciples were us—wildly, wickedly, wonderfully human.

I am not sure how he knew, but I trust that Jesus made his decision on the basis of spiritual insight and intuition. I think he sensed that these were the right 12. I also suspect that he was determined to make any 12 he chose into a team of mercy and justice. Ultimately, I believe Jesus trusted his own power to inspire these 12 to become their very best selves.

Why Were They Such Lousy Friends?

I think Jesus may have asked this question a few times. The disciples were, in fact, very good friends. They were also very human. Jesus' friends were forced to deal with crisis after crisis. They faced daily ridicule and scorn. They knew their fair share of persecution. Under these trying circumstances, the disciples held up reasonably well.

We have all been disappointed by friends. We've all known the pain of betrayal or the disappointment of having a friend fail to meet our expectations. The disciples were just like us. They were often honest and true, devoted friends of Jesus. On a few rare occasions they proved to be a real disappointment. Overall, I would suspect that Jesus would have given them high marks as friends.

Where Were the Women?

Like so many of the women of history, they were in the background. Women were not allowed a prominent role in Jesus' ministry, or at least not one that was acknowledged as a disciple. The bottom line was that as a Jew, Jesus came from a patriarchal and male-dominated culture and faith. Women were not allowed leadership roles in the Temple or politics.

It is vital to note, however, that women did play a role in the ministry of Jesus. The Gospel of Luke makes it clear that not only did women follow Jesus, but in many respects, they were also the ones who performed much of his ministry. In the lovely little story of Martha and Mary (Luke 10:38–42), we are told that Jesus thought of both as close friends. This was shocking for the day. Jesus was on intimate terms with women, yet he was not married. This raised more than a few eyebrows.

It was women who first saw Jesus risen from the grave. This was probably no surprise to Jesus, as he clearly saw women as possessors of a deep and abiding faith.

I will go so far as to say that I believe there were women disciples. I acknowledge that Scripture does not lend credence to that conviction, but neither does it dismiss the possibility. It just seems likely that Jesus, a champion of equality and the outcast, would have considered some of his close female followers disciples. The fact that it is not recorded in Scripture may have more to do with the cultural and religious norms than with the wishes of Jesus.

A Bad Word

Many still argue that women should not be ordained. Scripture is once again hauled in to prove the point. Jesus chose 12 male disciples, didn't he? Well, either all the ordained women in the world today are liars and were not called by the Holy Spirit to ministry, or they are worthy of ordination. If the call is true, the ordination is true.

The Duties of a Disciple

Jesus was brutally honest. He did not mince words. He said what he meant, and he meant what he said. Jesus was clear on his expectations of a disciple. The job description was formidable—even a bit frightening. These 12 men knew what it meant to be true to their calling as disciples. They knew it meant a way of thinking and behaving, an attitude and perspective, and a set of convictions and beliefs.

Here is what might be called a job description for being a disciple of Jesus:

- **Mature.** A disciple of Jesus must be capable of handling conflict, enduring hardship, and weathering a crisis. (Matthew 10:38–39)

- **Loving.** A disciple is expected to be extravagant in his loving. Disciples must love the tough to love—even their enemies. Disciples must love until it hurts. (John 13:34–35)

- **Compassionate.** A disciple must allow another person's tears to roll down his cheeks. (Matthew 11:28–30)

- **Forgiving.** A disciple must offer no excuses for failing to forgive. A disciple must know full well that he is offering only that which Jesus first offered him. (Matthew 18:21–22)

- **Serving.** A disciple must be unafraid to kneel and wash a stranger's feet. (John 13:12–17)

- **Sacrificing.** A disciple must often choose another's needs over his own. (Luke 22:25–27)

- **Aware.** A disciple must be aware of the world around him. He must notice and pay attention. He must see the need, wants, and wishes of others. He must keep his eyes open to crimes of the heart. He must keep his heart open to signs of injustice. (Mark 8:17–18)

- **Followers.** A disciple must be willing to let Jesus lead. A disciple must surrender control of his life to God. No effort or energy is to be wasted trying to be in charge. (Matthew 16:24–27)

- **Faithful.** A disciple must pray, worship, study Scripture, and serve with discipline. A disciple must walk the walk of faith. (Matthew 10:16–42)

- **Joyful.** A disciple must know genuine happiness. He must laugh often. A disciple must receive each day as a gift. A disciple must be bloated with gratitude. (John 17:13–19)

- **Peacemaker.** A disciple must work daily to be at peace with self, others, nature, the world, and God. A disciple must abhor war of all kinds. (John 14:27–29)

- **Good actor.** A disciple must act like Jesus, to see life through Jesus' eyes, to hear as Jesus would hear, to be the very presence of Jesus whenever and wherever possible. A disciple must be a good actor. Daily one must play the role of Jesus, with the Bible as their script, the Holy Spirit their director, the world their stage. (John 15:1–17)

A disciple must have a bleeding heart. Yes, a bleeding heart. The core job of a disciple is to care, to feel compassion, to show mercy. The essence of discipleship is to heal the world. Healing requires a huge heart, a heart bursting with tenderness, a heart without calluses, a heart that knows pain and hurt and heartache, a heart that bleeds when suffering is witnessed.

A Ministry of Mercy

Following Jesus required a deep commitment to those who were suffering or in need. A disciple is not allowed the privilege of judging others. No questions are asked as to how a person got himself in a situation. Discipleship is not at all about tough love; it is about loving the tough to love.

Spread the Good Word

Then the King will say to those on the right, "Come, you who are blessed by my Father, inherit the Kingdom prepared for you from the foundation of the world. For I was hungry, and you fed me. I was thirsty, and you gave me drink. I was a stranger, and you invited me into your home. I was naked, and you gave me clothing. I was sick, and you cared for me. I was in prison, and you visited me."

The righteous ones will reply, "Lord, when did we ever see you hungry and feed you? Or thirsty and give you something to drink? Or a stranger and show you hospitality? Or naked and give you clothing? When did we ever see you sick or in prison, and visit you?" And the King will tell them, "I assure you, when you did it to one of the least of these my brothers and sisters you were doing it to me!"

—Matthew 25:37–40

Jesus instructed his disciples to remember that in serving others they were serving God, and in serving God they were serving themselves: when we share or care, offer a helping hand, intervene in an abusive situation, comfort a person in pain, or lift up the weak. We are ultimately helping ourselves. We are freeing ourselves to be the people we were meant to be. We are enabling ourselves to know satisfaction. We are creating a safer and saner world for us all.

The Courage of the First Disciples

In some ways I have not given the first disciples their due. Yes, they were ordinary and human, but they were also courageous. Imagine the strength of character it took to stand up and follow Jesus. Imagine how hard it had to have been to walk away from family and friends, to leave your dreams and goals behind, to uproot yourself from everything you know, and to follow a man named Jesus—who took them on a perilous journey to a cross.

My family wants me to be safe and secure. They want me to be popular. They even want me to be well respected and well known. I think this is normal. Our families want the best for us. By "best" they mean what makes our lives easy and materially well-off.

Jesus wants the opposite. He asks us to follow him, knowing full well that to do so will cause us pain and persecution. He is not at all interested in our fame or fortune, our power or popularity, or what we have achieved by the world's standards. He cares only about the depth and extent of our loving and forgiving.

Make no mistake about it. To get up and follow Jesus was no small achievement for the first disciples. It was a huge risk. It made for many furious families. I would bet that the mothers and fathers of the disciples held Jesus in quite low regard—at least initially.

The disciples all came from traditional homes. Family was to be placed on a pedestal. In Jewish homes parents were to be revered. To show honor to one's family was an expectation. Jesus asked his disciples to break every rule in the book when it came to family. He asked them to choose him first! And they did! On that quality alone, the disciples have earned my respect.

Spread the Good Word

Your enemies will be right in your own household! If you love your father or mother more than you love me, you are not worthy of being mine; or if you love your son or daughter more than me, you are not worthy of being mine. If you cling to your life, you will lose it; but if you give it up for me, you will find it.

—Matthew 10:36–39

The Least You Need to Know

- The disciples were 12 men chosen by Jesus to be his team ministry.
- These disciples were ordinary men who proved to be quite human.
- Jesus celebrated great diversity in his selections.
- A disciple is expected to be mature, loving, compassionate, forgiving, serving, sacrificing, aware, willing to follow, faithful, joyful, and a peacemaker.
- The core of being a disciple is to act as if you are in the presence of Jesus, the presence of mercy.

Part 5

Christian Scripture: Jesus' Ministry

As a minister, I marvel at how similar ministry is today to what Jesus outlined for his disciples back then.

Ministry requires good preaching. Preaching is the means by which a minister inspires and guides his or her flock. Preaching declares the vision of a ministry. A good sermon must reach the heart. When Jesus preached, he was trying to transform human hearts.

Ministry is also about healing. Binding the brokenhearted. Comforting those who are alone, lost, or hurting for whatever reason. Ministry is the work of compassion and mercy. It is the offering of grace and forgiveness. Jesus literally performed miracles of healing.

Ministry is also about playing prophet. At times a minister must shake things up. He or she must challenge their flock to see the spiritual failure of their ways. Prophets make folks angry, jar them loose from complacency, and make things happen. Jesus was a pure prophet. He turned the world on its ear.

I let my congregation know on a regular basis that I am their minister, and not the ministry. They are the ministry. I believe Jesus did the same with his disciples—and in so doing passed that message onto all who choose to call themselves Christian. We are all ministers!

Chapter 12

Jesus the Preacher: The Sermon on the Mount

In This Chapter

- Preaching is a minister's means of inspiration
- Jesus' Sermon on the Mount established the vision of his ministry
- The Beatitudes formed the basis of the Christian message and the heart of Jesus' ministry
- The Sermon on the Mount addressed vital human issues
- Jesus offered guidance on how to live a fruitful and faithful life

I am sure Jesus gave many sermons, short, devotional pep talks to his disciples, meaningful addresses to his followers, or the occasional spontaneous speech or sermon at an impromptu gathering. But Jesus also had one main sermon—the Sermon on the Mount. Here Jesus presented to his disciples and a gathered throng the essence of his message, the heart of his ministry.

On the side of a mountain, Jesus is said to have delivered a sermon that inspired hearts and minds, provoked scorn and ridicule from the religious elite, and challenged all listeners to a new way of living.

As you read this chapter, you will gain clarity on the importance of Jesus' Sermon on the Mount. The Beatitudes, a key section of the sermon, make it clear that discipleship is much more about *being* than *doing*. Within this sermon we hear the major themes that will dominate the remainder of Jesus' life and ministry. The Sermon on the Mount is the equivalent of a statement of purpose. It is here that Jesus outlines the mission of the Christian faith.

The Beatitudes = the Being Attitudes (Matthew 5:1–11)

I recently conducted a worship for youth in which I asked the group to tell me the qualities of an American success story. I told them that I wanted to know what they believed is required in America to gain happiness and success on a personal and professional basis. What does a person living the good life look like?

The responses came fast and furious. Within five minutes we had composed the following top 10 list of necessary qualities to attain the good life in America:

- Good looks; sexually attractive
- Good in school; good grades
- Good athlete
- Popular; prominent positions in clubs, etc.
- Attends a good college
- Comes from a good home
- Knows the right people in the right positions
- Has strong financial backing; investors
- Is competitive; a winner
- Is ambitious; knows how to play the game and climb the ladder

This list was composed in a very ho-hum fashion. The group spoke of these qualities as being obvious ones. When we looked together at the list, there was no real reaction from the group other than a shrug, as if everyone knew this to be true.

Can you imagine what Jesus might have to say about such a list?

Are these the qualities he would be looking for? No matter how much or little you know about Jesus, I would guess you know the answer to this line of questioning. The answer is just as obvious as the ones that formed the youth group's success list.

When Jesus preached the Beatitudes, he was preaching to people who had been raised on a certain set of beliefs. His disciples and followers were fed on a steady diet of hearing that if you were blessed by God you were happy, healthy, wealthy, and wise.

If you were cursed by God, you were sick, poor, in the midst of crisis, and a social reject or outcast. Jesus' listeners on that mountainside had long believed that if they were obedient to God, they would be blessed and that their curses were to be understood as a sign of their disobedience.

With this in mind, take a look at to whom and for what Jesus offered blessings:

- Blessed are those who are needy for God. Dependent.
- Blessed are those who mourn. Grieve.
- Blessed are those who are gentle and lowly. Losers.
- Blessed are those who are passionate about justice. Those with strong convictions.
- Blessed are those who could care less about worldly success. Losers.
- Blessed are those who are merciful. Tender-hearted. Bleeding hearts.
- Blessed are those who are pure in heart. Honest. Loyal. Devoted.
- Blessed are those who are peacemakers. Reconcilers. Compromisers. Celebrators of diversity.
- Blessed are those who are persecuted. Social misfits or outcasts. Rejects. Geeks. Nerds. Losers.

Jesus offered blessings to everyone the world despises. Jesus offered blessings for all those qualities that the world would label "loser." Can you see why it is so difficult to genuinely choose to follow Jesus?

The Sermon on the Mount ironically began with a conclusion. The Beatitudes state clearly what Jesus valued, believed to be of vital importance, and passionately cared about. The Beatitudes outline a framework of blessings that certainly does not promise a follower an easy life. In fact, just the opposite. It offers the guarantee of crisis, conflict, bitter loss, and moments of being scorned, even mocked, for what one believes.

Jesus opened his sermon with the tough stuff. He told his disciples and followers that to follow him would require a strong and loving heart, an open and honest mind, and a soul convinced that God's will must be followed. The life of faith is a grueling and gracious process of maturation. The building of the Kingdom is painstaking work. To claim Jesus as the Messiah, our Lord, means to turn one's back on what the world thinks. Jesus was a fearless preacher!

The Good Word

In America you are what you do. Your identity is directly connected with what you do for a living. American success is all about doing. Just do it. Do it until you are satisfied. Those are fitting American mantras. Jesus is concerned with what you are *being*. Are you being kind, patient, gentle, loving, forgiving, and merciful? Jesus cares not about what you have accomplished—your *doing*—but what he can accomplish through you—your *being*. Here's the trick: What Jesus values will not pay you money or win you power or prestige. It will only make you a good person. A good neighbor. A good friend. A good mate. A good Christian. It will only bring you a life of satisfaction and joy.

Grace and the Law

Jesus also used the Sermon on the Mount to clear up a misunderstanding. Jesus often challenged the religious elite, especially the Pharisees, about the Law. For this reason it was assumed that he was opposed to the Law. Nothing could have been further from the truth.

Jesus had great love and respect for the Law, but he did warn his followers not to worship the Law. What? Jesus felt that many religious leaders were spending so much time trying to keep to the letter of the Law—to be perfect—that they were losing touch with the spirit of the Law. The Law was and is an excellent means of keeping one's heart and mind focused on God. Jesus affirms this. If, however, adhering to the Law becomes obsessive, even fanatic, then even the Law can become spiritually destructive.

The pursuit of perfection is always demoralizing and futile—as well as physically, emotionally, and spiritually destructive.

A Bad Word

The Law can become obsessive. The Pharisees were more concerned with keeping the Law perfectly than about being people who demonstrated mercy and justice. The Law without love has no meaning. Even today, many religious folks are so busy memorizing Bible verses or spouting doctrine and dogma, that they have no time or energy left to love their neighbor as their self.

In simplest terms, Jesus advocates grace above the Law. Grace is the unconditional love of God. It is eternal and endless forgiveness. For Christians, Jesus is the event of grace. Though the Law—ceremonial, civil, and moral—can be a worthy means of loving God with your whole being, it is grace that best keeps us centered in Christ.

Jesus was often angry with the Pharisees, yet he also clearly loved the Pharisees. He felt great intimacy with these religious scholars. His anger was fueled by his disappointment. He expected great things from them but witnessed an absence of genuine faith. He saw the Pharisees as people who had become so consumed with trying to meet every detail of the Law that they had completely lost the essence of the Law—love and mercy.

> But I warn you—unless you obey God better than the teachers of religious law and the Pharisees do, you can't enter the Kingdom of Heaven at all!
>
> —Matthew 5:17–20

Jesus went so far as to call the Pharisees whitewashed tombs. He said that they looked clean and shiny on the outside, but inside were filled with a dead man's bones. The Pharisees had a dead faith, a faith with no graciousness, a loveless faith, a faith that loved through gritted teeth. (Matthew 23:25–26)

A Bad Word

Read the Gospel of Matthew 23:1–36. This is a scathing indictment of those who are thought to be experts in the Law. Jesus said that they knew the Law but did not live it. He called them hypocrites, religious phonies, hard-hearted souls. The Pharisees knew the Law but failed to be touched by grace. Untouched by grace, they lived lives of self-righteous boasting. They became most un-Godlike.

Handling Hard Emotions

Jesus was a tough counselor. The Sermon on the Mount offered tough advice on how to handle some of life's difficult emotions:

- **Anger.** He stated clearly that we cannot worship with anger in our hearts. Before we worship, we need to clean the anger out of our systems. (Matthew 5:21–26)

- **Lust.** Jesus made a tricky emotion even more difficult to handle. He told his followers that lust itself constitutes adultery. Ouch! I think this is God's way of warning us not to play with fire. (Matthew 5:27–30)

- **Revenge.** Turn the other cheek. Don't even think about getting even. There is no such thing. Getting even only distances you further from God. Turn the other cheek = turn it over to God. (Matthew 5:38–42)

Jesus offered no easy answers. He told us to pray to be stronger people. Religion is about trying to be perfect. Faith is about embracing imperfection. Religion is often used as a means of declaring moral superiority. Faith is always used as a way of affirming spiritual equality. Religion is usually a lot of rules and regulations—don'ts. Faith is a lot of love and mercy—do's. Religion is frequently smug and self-righteous. Faith is humbling. Religion is often used to judge others. Faith is used only in judging oneself. Religion often takes us far from God. Faith always brings us back home.

Vows and Commitments (Matthew 5:31–37)

The times in which Jesus ministered were filled with treachery and deceit. Lying was commonplace. Cheating was an everyday occurrence. Often the religious leaders were no more than scam artists. Sound familiar?

Jesus used the occasion of the Sermon on the Mount to challenge his listeners to be true to their word, to fulfill their commitments, and to practice loyalty in all relationships. He strongly advocated faithfulness for marriage partners and admonished couples to avoid divorce.

Jesus spoke simply on this issue. He stated that honesty is the foundation upon which all good relationships are built. Keeping it honest will keep it true.

Faithful and Fruitful

The Sermon on the Mount speaks directly on how to be faithful.
Jesus made it plain that a faithful life is one lived simply and quietly.
A person's faith is not for show, to prove a point, or to be competi-
tive in any way. True faith gives witness by action.

Faith has no need for affirmation or attention. Faith seeks only the
approval of God. Jesus highlights the following as key aspects of a
faithful life:

- Giving to the needy is expected. This giving should be
  anonymous. God will know! (Matthew 6:1–4)

- Prayer is encouraged but should be simple and private. There
  is no need for showy or wordy prayers. (Matthew 6:5–6)

- Fasting is encouraged but again not as a religious show.
  Fasting should simply be a means of focusing oneself on one's
  dependence on God. (Matthew 6:16–18)

- Keep on seeking. Faith is a process of seeking and finding.
  Jesus tutored his listeners on the importance of being relent-
  less in pursuit of God. Jesus also made it clear that God will
  not turn his back on anyone who passionately seeks him.
  Keep on treating others as you would have them treat you.
  God will notice. (Matthew 7:7–12)

- Build your life on the solid foundation of obedience.
  (Matthew 7:21–27)

As for being fruitful and successful in the eyes of God, Jesus saw
this as solely a matter of compassion. The Sermon on the Mount
makes it abundantly clear that compassion is the first fruit of faith.
Compassion is not pity. Compassion is not self-denial.

Compassion is truly identifying with the needy. Compassion is sharing the suffering of another human being. Compassion is to mo-
mentarily be possessed of the heart of God.

The Sermon on the Mount preaches a message that sees compassion as the core of the Christian way of life.

Money Matters (Matthew 6:19–24)

The Sermon on the Mount makes assumptions. One assumption is that folks of faith know that money is in competition with God for worship. Money demands worship. Greed can become a form of worship.

Being addicted to accumulation can become the liturgy of life. Money or God? That is the central choice of faith, the acid test of faith, the crucial decision of the disciple. Jesus was 100 percent clear. Money challenges God for time, energy, and the investment of the soul. You can't serve both!

The number-one social issue in America is greed. It is greed that leads to oppression. Greed is the catalyst for the chasm growing between rich and poor. Greed is at the heart of the mean-spiritedness we witness everywhere. Some TV evangelists even try to make it sound like Jesus was big on bucks, that he was an advocate of profiteering. Jesus is even portrayed as a first-class capitalist. Jesus was opposed to capitalism. He did not believe in private property. Jesus lived in such a way that if he had two coats, he would give one away. Everything was God's property. The church has a horrid struggle trying to remain true to what Jesus did say about money!

The Good Word

Imagine how beautiful it would be to go through one day without the need to judge anyone. Imagine the freedom to be found in going through a whole day without being judged by anyone. Imagine the calm. Imagine the energy otherwise wasted on trying to please others and avoid judgment. Imagine the pleasure we would give Jesus.

Judgementalness (Matthew 7:1–6)

Jesus despised the judgementalness of the religious elite. He loathed how they felt morally superior. He hated their self-righteous attitude and behavior.

> Take the log out of your eye before you try to point out the speck in somebody else's.
>
> —Matthew 7:3–5

How direct could he get? How much clearer could he make it? Judgementalness is spiritually unacceptable.

Worry Warts (Matthew 6:25–34)

Jesus told his listeners that a faithful life, a fruitful existence, is free of worry. There is no need to worry about how you look, sound, or come across. There is no need to be concerned with either image or impression. A person of faith puts his complete trust in God.

> Therefore do not be anxious about tomorrow, for tomorrow will be anxious for itself. Let the day's own trouble be sufficient for the day.
>
> —Matthew 6:34

The God who knows you inside out will take care of your needs. There is no reason to try and control the day. Trust the day. Surrender to it. Rejoice in it. Let it be. God will provide.

The Sermon on the Mount is magnificent. It is clear and compelling. It is direct and to the point. It is easy to understand, at least to the faithful heart. It pulls no punches. It plays no tricks. This is a sermon that tells it exactly like it is—or should I say, like it should be.

Jesus gave one main sermon. Upon that single effort all other sermons have been based.

The Least You Need to Know

- The Sermon on the Mount captures the essence of Jesus' ministry.

- The Beatitudes offer blessing to those folks the world rejects.

- Jesus preached about the importance of keeping to the spirit of the Law—mercy and justice and equality.

- Jesus encouraged his listeners to discipline their faith: giving to the needy, praying, fasting, obeying God's will, and avoiding greed, judgementalness, and needless worrying at all costs.

- Jesus kept the message simple: Ground your faith in grace and keep compassion at the center of your life.

Chapter 13

Jesus as Teacher: The Parables

In This Chapter

- A parable is a small story that teaches a big lesson
- Jesus taught his disciples and followers with parables
- Jesus taught many parables about how a little, in matters of faith, can be more than enough
- Jesus taught many parables about the importance of finding those in society who are lost
- Jesus taught many parables about how the Kingdom of God would look nothing like the world

Jesus taught his disciples and followers with parables. A parable is a many-sided story. It is a story that contains a moral lesson, that reveals a spiritual truth.

On the surface, a parable appears to be a simple story taken from daily life. But upon reflection, we begin to see a parallel story taking place beneath the surface. This story is not hidden, but can be seen as if you were looking through ice—not as clear, but certainly there for the grasping.

As you read this chapter, you will gain a deep appreciation for why Jesus chose to teach in parables. You will gain insight into the power of a parable to capture an eternal truth. You will witness how Jesus utilizes parables to gently teach often troubling lessons. This chapter will clarify some of the prominent messages of the parables: the importance of reaching out to the outcast, the call to celebrate God's standards and not the world's, the challenge to build the Kingdom of God on this earth.

What Is a Parable?

Jesus taught in parables because people remember stories. A good story speaks straight to the heart. It captures the mind by using everyday images, and it ignites the imagination by stirring the soul to wonder. A good story can be unforgettable—and most are.

All of Jesus' parables emanate from the ordinary lives of the ordinary people who were his followers. His stories were grounded in the soil and in the lives of those who farmed and waited for the gifts of rain and harvest. Many of his stories reflected the wide gap that existed in Jesus' world between rich and poor. Many lifted up those who his world hated—in particular the Samaritan.

A parable teaches on many levels. A parable can be used personally, with all characters, images, and symbols being used to speak exclusively to the self. A parable can speak to a community of faith and be taken as addressing the concerns of those spiritually focused. A parable can speak politically, socially, and economically and serve as the tool of the prophetic voice. A parable can speak to everyone, everywhere, eternally.

A good teacher uses what works and what has the best chance of conveying the subject to be taught. Parables did just that.

Jesus was an excellent teacher. His stories remain as true today as the first day they were told. These small stories made such big points that, to this day, their peaks continue to be revealed in poetry, literature, theater, film, and art.

Just a Pinch Is Plenty

Jesus' world was not all that different from our own, especially on a spiritual plane. The society in which Jesus ministered was big on big. The Temple had to be big and cost big bucks. The religious elite had to have big reputations. The Law had to be big and getting bigger. Miracles had to be the parting-of-the-sea kind. God had to be larger than life.

Jesus was, in all respects, a big disappointment. He wasn't big in any way. He had no big titles or positions. He had no big home or treasure chest. He had no big following, and the rabble that did trudge after him were a really odd collection of misfits, outcasts, and eccentrics. If Jesus was big in any way, he was a big loser—at least by every standard of the world.

Jesus used parables to teach important lessons. In matters of faith, less is more; a little is plenty; nothing can be everything. The following parables—swift and slight, a mere image—teach how faith transforms the small into huge.

It's Yeasting!

I recall watching my grandmother make homemade bread. I was fascinated with how a little yeast could make the dough rise to such epic proportions. As her designated bread-checker, I would often yell to her, "It's yeasting!" I would shout in awe at the magical rise of the bread.

Spread the Good Word

The Kingdom of Heaven is like yeast used by a woman making bread. Even though she used a large amount of flour, the yeast permeated every part of the dough.

—Matthew 13:33

Jesus was aware of the same magic of a pinch of faith. A pinch of faith could saturate a whole day and transform it from one of ugly bitterness to beautiful hope. Faith could convert a frown into a smile and a tear of sorrow into a laugh of joy, and give a life without meaning the experience of total satisfaction.

By comparing the Kingdom of God to yeast, Jesus made a big point with one little image—a heart and mind faithfully focused on building the Kingdom will create a whole new heart, mind, spirit, and being in the believer. One pinch of the Kingdom will permeate and bloat the soul with meaning and purpose.

The Pricey Pearl

The Kingdom of God is compared to a pearl. It is of such great value that it should be pursued and treasured above all else. Finding the pearl requires a search; the search must become the top priority.

> Again, the Kingdom of Heaven is like a pearl merchant on the lookout for choice pearls. When he discovered a pearl of great value, he sold everything he owned and bought it!
>
> —Matthew 13:45–46

Think of just how many truths are conveyed by these two quick lines—one slight parable:

- We must be on the lookout for that which is of value.
- We must search high and low for that which has eternal value.
- When we find it, we need to drop everything.
- To sell everything else is to make our faith, following Jesus, building the Kingdom—the singular priority of our lives.
- We are called to choose the road less traveled.
- We are called to get rid of that which is of no value.
- Faith requires a 100 percent investment.
- In God's eyes, the Kingdom is all that matters.

A little can say a lot!

Does Anyone Have Any Grey Poupon?

A mustard seed was as common to the people of Jesus' time as corn would be to the good folks of Nebraska. A mustard seed was probably the smallest of all seeds used by the farmers of the time. Though it has very small beginnings, it results in something quite large and lovely.

Spread the Good Word

The Kingdom of Heaven is like a mustard seed planted in a field. It is the smallest of all seeds, but it becomes the largest of garden plants and grows into a tree where birds can come and find shelter in its branches.

—Matthew 13:31–32

Small is beautiful. That is a message apparently lost on our American culture. Think about it. What a big difference can come from just a little laughter, a little kindness, a little honesty, or, especially, a little faith.

At times when I would start to sound cynical or whiney, my complaining beginning to sour the house, my deceased wife Christine would often say, "Hey, how about a little faith right now? Think that might help?" It was always the splash of cold, clean, refreshing water that I needed to snap out of it.

It's the Soil, Stupid!

Seeds. Faith is like seeds. Small and seemingly insignificant. Tiny glances and glimpses of grace. Moments of clarity that God is present. Experiences that take our breath away, leave us dumbstruck, or

give us a lump in the throat. Falling in love. Choosing to love.
Being in love. Forgiveness of any kind—giving or receiving. These
are the seeds of faith.

I tend to think of each day as sprinkling my life with these seeds.
The issue is whether or not I am receptive to having these seeds
planted in my soul. This is the exact same issue addressed by the
Parable of the Sower. In this parable Jesus pointed out that the
seeds of faith are abundant, but it is the condition of the soil that
determines the condition of the faith.

In the Parable of the Sower, the gardener or farmer, God, is planting seed. He finds four different soils:

- **The footpath.** This well-worn soil is hard as a rock. The
  seed will just sit on top of it, and the birds will come and eat
  the seed. This soil is like a hardened heart or a closed mind.
  Nothing can get in.

- **Shallow, rocky soil.** This is soil where there is no room for
  roots, like a soul that has no real room for faith. What little
  faith there is, is all talk. Without roots, this faith will wither
  and die in a crisis of any kind. This faith is like a shallow
  friend. You can't count on it, and you would be wise to place
  your trust elsewhere.

- **Thorny soil.** This is soil that symbolizes lives that are consumed with making money or being a big success, too busy
  trying to win the rat race to have any time for God. Since the
  rat race is won by rats, it is questionable if God would want
  them anyway.

- **Fertile soil.** This is soil that is open and receptive. It is soil
  that will welcome the seeds and nourish them with water and
  fertilizer. This is the individual who has an open heart, mind,
  and soul. This is a faith that will mature and grow strong.

Jesus was asking his followers to be like fertile soil. He was asking
them to open themselves up wide to the presence of God. He was
asking them to notice the seed that was being sprinkled on their day
and being. He wanted that seed to be planted, deep, where it could
grow strong roots, where it could be nourished by the grace of God.

Lost and Found

We have millions of homeless in America. Jesus would be appalled. Jesus was appalled. Jesus would not be challenging the homeless to get jobs to pay for homes. Jesus would be challenging those with homes to open their doors or to make it their job to build homes for these folks. Jesus never asked why a person was in bad shape. He just asked those who were in good shape to be good neighbors.

Jesus used several parables to stress the spiritual importance of finding those who are lost. He made it abundantly clear that it was the task of the faithful to bring home those who had wandered away, those who are lost. In the Kingdom, not one person is disposable, of little use, or to be forgotten, neglected, or ignored.

A Bad Word

Who are the lost in America? It is a list that is long and getting longer every day. The homeless. The aged. The mentally ill. The poor. The uneducated. The handicapped. The retarded. The victims of AIDS. Many, many, many people of color. It is an embarrassing list for the wealthiest nation on earth. It is evidence of a Christian population with, at best, a shallow-rooted faith.

The Lost Sheep (Luke 15:1–7)

One hundred sheep. One lost sheep. The world would say that 99 will do just fine. The rule of the Kingdom is to make finding the lost sheep the top priority.

The Lost Coin (Luke 15:8–10)

A woman had 10 valuable coins. She lost one. Again, the world would say that nine would get her what she needed. The Kingdom would say that this is not the point. She was given all 10, now she must find the one that is lost. Each coin is of equal value. Do not waste the treasure God has given you.

The Lost Son (Luke 15:11–32)

This is probably the most famous of all parables. The theme is the same, but the story is more detailed and involved. The parable flows as follows:

- A young son gets bored with work on the family farm.
- He tells his dad to drop dead. He wants his inheritance now.
- His father gives him his inheritance.
- The young man goes off to the big city to make a name for himself.
- He squanders his fortune on loose living and becomes a real party animal.
- A famine hits the area, and the young man is hungry and poor.
- At a pig trough, he hits his spiritual bottom.
- He comes to his senses and heads home. He realizes that even the servants at home eat better than pig feed.
- Walking down the road, he sees his father sprinting to meet him.
- The father throws a huge party for the whole neighborhood in celebration of his son's return.
- The young man's older brother is livid. Why didn't he get a party? He was the one who was responsible and stayed at home and worked the farm. What about him?
- The father explains that he is celebrating his young son's return. Being at home with his father should have been a daily celebration for the older son.

People of faith have always struggled with the notion of celebrating those who have made huge mistakes or show gaping flaws in their character. Jesus made celebrating forgiveness the crux of the Christian faith.

Celebrating forgiveness = the lost are now found

People of true faith, mature faith, have no need for recognition; they know their lives are blessed on a daily basis. A mature faith is thrilled to see someone lost come home to the grace of God.

The Upside of Down

Jesus had a vision of the Kingdom of God. His vision was not what the world would or did expect. In fact, his vision was the opposite of what the world expected. Jesus knew that this message would be offensive. He was aware of the hostility such thinking would receive—especially from the religious elite.

Jesus often shared this vision in the form of parables. These stories may appear to be harmless on the surface, but when embraced in their spiritual fullness, they cause the world genuine pain. It is within these parables that Jesus issued a direct challenge to the beliefs of the religious elite.

Jesus was offensive. Jesus infuriated his culture. Jesus set forth a blistering attack and challenge to the religious elite of his time. The Jesus preached in much of America today is anything but offensive. He sounds like a white, southern, Republican, American, a good businessman in a blue suit with a white shirt and a burgundy tie. Trust me. Were Jesus to come today, he would not live in the suburbs. He would not work on Wall Street. He might not minister in America at all. Wherever he would be, it would be with the poor and needy. It is tragic that we have tried to make Jesus so appealing, so popular, no more than a friendly superhero. He was anything but.

The Loser Banquet (Luke 14:15–24)

Let me review with you the story line of this parable, as well as unpack its symbols:

- God prepares a banquet.
- God sends Jesus out with a bunch of invitations.
- Jesus first invites the religious elite to the party.
- The religious elite have all kinds of excuses for not attending.
- Jesus issues a second round of invitations.

- Jesus invites misfits, outcasts, and those the world would view as lost or cursed or both. Losers.

- The banquet is held without the religious elite in attendance.

This parable is obvious. The world would expect that if God were to come and spend time on earth, he would devote his time to the good religious people. God does come. Jesus arrived but was not welcomed by the religious establishment. He found his home with those who were not religious, who did not know the Torah, and who could not or did not attend Temple. God threw a banquet for the very people the world believed God to have cursed.

The Good Samaritan (Luke 10:25–37)

First you need to understand something. The idea of a good Samaritan was a repulsive idea to the religious establishment of Jesus' time. Samaritans were despised. They were seen as spiritually soiled. In America today, a Samaritan would be the equivalent of a gay, black, female, drug addict with AIDS—and a bleeding-heart liberal at that.

This parable is a real slap in the face to the religious elite.

Let me summarize both the contents of the parable and the lessons taught:

- A Jew is traveling to Jericho and is attacked by bandits.

- He is left beaten, stripped, and robbed by the side of the road.

- A Jewish priest walks right on by.

- A Temple assistant walks right on by.

- A Samaritan stops and attends to all of the man's needs.

- The Samaritan shows the Jew extravagant mercy.

- The Samaritan takes the man to an inn, and he pays the bill.

- The Samaritan leaves but first promises to pay any further bill needed in caring for the beaten Jew.

- The Samaritan proves to be most God-like.

- The religious establishment once again fails.

Jesus pulled no punches. The religious people were too busy being religious to even notice the man in need at the side of the road. The Samaritan, the subject of Jewish scorn, came to the rescue. Jesus lifted up the Samaritan as a spiritual role model and hero. The world would be shocked by such a story. The religious establishment stunned. It was not a tale that told an easy-to-swallow truth.

The Good Word

Can you imagine your family throwing a feast for the poor and needy in your area? Can you imagine a Thanksgiving supper in your home with the seated guests being the homeless, the mentally ill, the nearby residents of a drug treatment center or a prison half-way house? Jesus was offensive. His challenges were extreme and tough.

The Parable of Wages (Matthew 20:1–16)

I can think of no other story in all of Scripture that would be more offensive to American culture—even religion. This parable teaches that those who have toiled all day in the vineyard will get the same exact pay as those who only work one hour. Just what is it that Jesus meant by such a story?

- He meant that God does not measure as the world measures.
- He meant that we do not earn God's love or forgiveness.
- He meant that everyone is worthy of God's grace.
- He meant that the religious establishment has no special rank or privilege in the Kingdom of God.
- He meant that the Kingdom of God is an equal opportunity employer.
- He meant God has no favorites.
- He meant God loves even those who the world hates.

Equality is one of the toughest principles of faith to believe in. It is even trickier to practice. Somehow we still want to measure faith. We want faith to be competitive. We want winners and losers.

Jesus celebrated the value of each and every individual on the planet. Each person is a child of God. Each is beloved. This is the nature of grace.

The Good Word

Do you recognize that in the eyes of God, a child who wallows in poverty in Calcutta is of equal value to you? Do you live with that in heart and mind? What difference does such a perspective make?

Plenty of Parables

Parables were Jesus' primary teaching device. They are abundant in the Gospels. They are only found in the Gospels. They are only found in Christian Scripture. I offer the following as a means of tracking the parables of Christian Scripture. Note which parables reoccur in more than one Gospel and which are exclusive to a particular Gospel. This will help you see the interrelatedness of the Gospels as well as the editorial vision and perspective of each.

The Gospel of Matthew:

> The Parable of the Four Soils (13:1–23)
> The Parable of the Weeds (13:24–30)
> The Parable of the Mustard Seed (13:31–32)
> The Parable of the Yeast (13:33–35)
> The Parable of the Hidden Treasure (13:44)
> The Parable of the Pearl Merchant (13:45–46)
> The Parable of the Fishing Net (13:45–52)
> The Parable of the Unforgiving Debtor (18:21–35)

The Parable of the Vineyard Workers (20:1–16)
The Parable of the Two Sons (21:28–32)
The Parable of the Evil Farmers (21:33–46)
The Parable of the Wedding Dinner (22:1–14)
The Parable of the Ten Bridesmaids (25:1–13)
The Parable of the Loaned Money (25:14–30)

The Gospel of Mark:

The Parable of the Four Soils (4:1–25)
The Parable of the Growing Seed (4:26–29)
The Parable of the Mustard Seed (4:30–34)
The Parable of the Evil Farmers (12:1–12)

The Gospel of Luke:

The Parable of the Four Soils (8:4–18)
The Parable of the Good Samaritan (10:25–37)
The Parable of the Rich Fool (12:13–21)
The Parable of the Lost Sheep (15:1–7)
The Parable of the Lost Coin (15:8–10)
The Parable of the Lost Son (15:11–32)
The Parable of the Shrewd Manager (16:1–18)
The Parable of the Persistent Widow (18:1–8)
The Parable of the Two Men Who Prayed (18:9–14)
The Parable of the King's 10 Servants (19:11–27)
The Parable of the Evil Farmers (20:9–19)

The Gospel of John:

None recorded.

The parables are unique to Christian Scripture and are found only in the Gospels of Matthew, Mark, and Luke. Matthew used many parables in stating his case that Jesus had come so be the Messiah, first for the Jews, next for everyone else—the Gentiles. Luke's parables helped convey his message that Jesus was the champion of the poor and the outcast. John chose to use metaphoric images and symbols rather than parables. In the Gospel of John, Jesus was likened to the Bread of Life, Everflowing Streams, the Vine, the Good Shepherd, and the Way.

The Least You Need to Know

- Parables were a key teaching tool for Jesus.
- Parables are little stories that make a big point.
- Jesus used parables to stress that a little faith can move mountains.
- Jesus used parables to stress that people of faith are directly responsible and accountable for the lost of society.
- Jesus used parables to stress that the Kingdom of God would be no Disney World.
- Jesus used parables to stress that the Kingdom would be a place of equality, justice, and abundant mercy.

Chapter 14

Jesus as Healer: The Miracles

In This Chapter

- Jesus was a healer
- Jesus' disciples and followers saw healings as miracles
- Healings require faith; faith is the opposite of fear
- Jesus healed individuals who were thought to be possessed by demons
- Jesus displayed miraculous powers intended to heal the world

I approach all of life as a miracle. The entire Creation story leaves me breathless every single day. I am in awe of the majesty and mystery that is the universe—the one that flows inside my body as well as the one that spins by outside it. It all can give me a thick coating of goose bumps.

Now what about healings? Are healings miracles? How do I deal with the idea of Jesus as healer? How did Jesus manage to restore sight to the blind, enable the lame to walk and the deaf to hear, and rid folks troubled with mental illness of their demons? Could Jesus really raise people from the dead?

As you read this chapter, you will examine some of the miracles of Jesus documented in Scripture. You will learn of Jesus' healings. You will be told of the power of faith and forgiveness to heal. These healings are of both physical and mental illness—the latter being described as possession by demons. You will be asked to wrestle with the mystery of a miracle. You will be challenged to open your heart and mind to the reality of healings.

Can Miracles Really Happen?

I have no answers, no proofs, no boastful claims of faith. No words are adequate to the task. I just don't know. I do know that as a minister, I have heard tell of more than my fair share of healings. I have listened to accounts of events easily labeled miraculous. I have not encountered any such experiences or events in my own life—other than in the listening or reading.

Just a little over a year ago, I found myself praying like mad for a miracle. My wife fell into a coma after complications from surgery. I never got my miracle—sometimes God says no. Was God punishing me? God forbid, was Christine being punished? Was God determined to leave my son Justin without a mother? Was this God's crazy plan? Had my prayers gone unnoticed, or worse yet, did they fall on deaf ears? I had no answers, just my pain, anger, sadness, and grief.

After 16 months of grieving I can honestly say I am at a new place. I am still sad, but not as often. My anger has all but disappeared. I have come to an acceptance. I accept that life includes death. Every day we are living, we are also dying. I have come to realize that to receive the gift, I have to accept the whole package.

What changed in me? I believe it was my faith. My faith grew. It matured. I came to a new understanding. God's will includes death. I could accept—but not on any logical or rational basis—that all of life is a gift, even death. I may not know why we die, but I can trust that God's grace is from beginning to end and beyond. Death can claim no victory over faith.

My faith opened my eyes to a new awareness. God is not about blessings or curses. God is about grace. All is grace. Every moment of this life of ours is coated in grace, even the sad and tragic moments. Yes, even death.

In faith, I can comprehend the healings performed by Jesus. I feel no need to explain or defend them. I simply let them inform and illuminate my life and faith. Some things must be believed to be seen. I think of healings in this manner. I accept them as gospel truth.

There is no record of such healings in the Hebrew Scripture. There are miraculous events galore, but no such personal healings. This is unique to the Christian Scripture. This is exclusive to Jesus.

I believe there are many ways one can legitimately approach a healing or miracle:

- As a concrete physical fact and literal truth.
- As a sign of the power of faith to heal.
- As a sign of the power of God.
- As more of an emotional healing—especially in terms of forgiveness—which yields physical healing as well.
- As a spiritual transformation, which produces a physical transformation as well.
- As an unexplained mystery.

I would suspect that many of the healings performed by Jesus during his ministry were compilations of several encounters between Jesus and "patient," the cure often being a process rather than some magic-wand moment. Still, even there, I cannot say for sure. Anything is possible—in faith.

Miracles vs. Fear

Fear is the opposite of faith. Fear expects the worst. Faith expects the best. Fear seeks to rob faith of power. Fear strives to paralyze the spirit, to keep it from maturation. Fear seeks to keep the heart focused on that which does not matter. Fear wants a mind that is cluttered with worry, a mind that is either marooned in "oughts" of the past or the "what ifs" of the future.

Think about it. In your own life, how often has fear paralyzed you? Maybe not physically, but certainly emotionally or spiritually? Have you ever been sick with fear—worried sick?

Have you ever had an upset stomach from anxiety or a bad headache from stress? Fear can play havoc with the body.

Dis-ease. Out of ease. Fear creates a state of being un-easy.

Fear creates dis-ease.

Faith creates a sense of calm. Faith creates peace of heart and mind. Faith restores ease to the body. Faith heals.

Jesus ignited faith. He inspired it. He embraced people with grace. In Jesus, people experienced the fullness of love and forgiveness. In Jesus, they came to know a deep inner peace and a strength of soul. The power of Jesus' presence was in itself healing. It could mend a broken heart or spirit. It could bring a soul in despair back to life. It could grant the courage to change, forgive, or be forgiven. The presence of Jesus was transforming—physically, emotionally, and spiritually.

Faith creates a sense of calm. Faith creates peace of heart and mind. Faith restores ease to the body. Faith heals.

The Paralyzed Man (Mark 2:1–12)

Four men brought a paralyzed man on a mat to Jesus. They found the home where Jesus was staying packed with visitors. Finding no way to enter the house, the four men lifted the paralyzed man to the roof and lowered him down through a hole they made in the roof.

Jesus was impressed with their determination—faith. They were convinced that Jesus could heal—faith. They went to any lengths to get the paralyzed man to see Jesus—faith. Seeing this great display of faith, Jesus told the man that his sins were forgiven.

The man rose and walked.

Spread the Good Word

Seeing their faith, Jesus said to the paralyzed man, "My son, your sins are forgiven."

—Mark 2:5

Forgiveness is amazing. It has such healing powers. A soul consumed in guilt, saturated with shame, is diseased. Maybe physically. Maybe emotionally or relationally. Certainly spiritually. Forgiveness plays a prominent role in Jesus' miracle stories. Forgiveness is often the medicine that precedes the cure. Think about it. Remember the last time you felt fully forgiven for a transgression? Remember how wonderfully alive you felt? The power of forgiveness to heal and restore is real.

The Healing at the Pool (John 5:1–18)

This is a strange little story. Let me unpack its contents:

- A man was laying by the pool of Bethesda, a pool known to have miraculous healing powers.

- The healing powers of the pool were thought to be released when the water was stirred up.

- This man had been waiting to be lifted into the pool for 38 years; for 38 years he could not find help; for 38 years someone beat him into the rippling waters.

- Jesus *noticed* the man.

- Jesus asked if the man truly wished to walk. Jesus *cared* about his plight.

- Jesus did not help him into the pool; Jesus simply healed the man; the water was not necessary.

- Faith created this healing.

Jesus saw a man who had sought healing for 38 years, but not in the right place. It is faith in God that yields healing, not stirred up water. Jesus rewarded the lame man for his persistent search for wholeness—his steadfast search of 38 years.

The Roman Officer's Servant (Luke 7:1–10)

The servant of a Roman officer in charge of 100 men was sick and near death. Somehow, the Roman officer came to believe that the Jews were God's chosen people. He had grown in his love and respect for the Jews and had even built them a synagogue. Normally, Jews would have held a Roman officer in contempt.

This Roman officer does not come to Jesus, nor does he expect Jesus to come to him. As an officer, he knew that his soldiers would follow an order whether or not he were present. Likewise, he was certain that Jesus could heal his servant even if he wasn't present. He had faith in the power of Jesus to heal. He did not need to see to believe.

Jesus was amazed at the depth and maturity of the Gentile's faith. Jesus stated that he had not seen such a faith among the Jews. The Roman officer's servant was found healed. Once again, faith was the catalyst for healing. It was faith alone that unleashed Jesus' healing powers.

Spread the Good Word

When Jesus heard this, he was amazed. Turning to the crowd, he said, "I tell you, I haven't seen faith like this in all the land of Israel!" And when the officer's friends returned to his house, they found the slave completely healed.

—Luke 7:9–10

I am struck by the love and loyalty of the Roman officer for his servant. This devotion may not have cured the servant, but it must have given him cause to trust the officer's faith in Jesus.

Miracles vs. Demons

Demons. What a powerful little word. It conjures up horror-movie images. It is a term associated with Satan and exorcisms, a concept filled with fear, the complete loss of control to a force outside oneself. I think of demons as a mental illness, as going crazy, as schizophrenia, as psychosis.

All forms of mental illness existed in Jesus' time, just as they do now. Even today, people have a hard time accepting the reality that someone may hear voices or have more than one personality. Trust me—mental illness is real, just as genuine as any physical ailment. Even when I hear people say, "It is all in their head," I want to say, "Yes, that is where all mental illness is located."

Jesus healed mental illness. He rid the soul of demons. He did so in two primary ways:

- **Touch.** Jesus physically touched mentally ill individuals. He was unafraid of embracing them with love. He touched their hearts. He touched them deeply, and left them deeply touched. In a world that would not go near a person possessed by demons, Jesus walked right in and offered healing touch.

- **Forgiveness.** Guilt can drive a person crazy. The anxiety and stress of shame can make a person insane. To hear the gracious words of forgiveness spoken to you was a true catalyst for healing. To feel and know that one is forgiven was capable of restoring sanity. Forgiveness is the great exterminator of demons.

A Boy and His Demon (Matthew 17:14–21)

Here is a case of mistaken identity. Epilepsy was thought to be possession by demons. Epilepsy had to have been terrifying to the people of Jesus' time. I am sure that most folks would have run away from anyone suffering an epileptic seizure. Jesus did not.

Jesus healed the afflicted boy. The father's faith was the catalyst for the healing. The father knelt before Jesus and begged for mercy for his son. I suspect that not only was Jesus impressed by this man's faith, but the son was as well. Could it be that witnessing his father's faith was what made the boy receptive to this miracle?

My Name Is Legion (Mark 5:1–20)

This is a famous story of demon possession. Let me summarize the essence of the story:

- A mentally ill man has been shunned by society.
- He is forced to live in a cave outside of town.
- He is totally alone. He is shackled.
- In isolation his insanity grows; his demons become legion (a legion being a division of Roman soldiers numbering 3,000 to 6,000).
- The man seeks out Jesus, and Jesus does not run away.
- Jesus feels great compassion for the man.
- Jesus can see the urgency of this man's pain.
- Jesus shows no fear; he greets the man with faith.
- Jesus listens to him explain his mental illness. He hears his confession.
- Jesus orders the demons out of the man and into a nearby herd of pigs.
- The man is healed.

This story is an exorcism. Jesus heard the man's confession, and he demanded that the demons be gone. He used the pigs, notoriously unclean animals for the Jews, to be the receptacles for the demons.

This is called transference. It is the same idea used by therapists when they have someone beat a pillow—the anger toward someone goes out onto the pillow.

The Good Word

Jesus touched the untouchable. He calmly approached individuals who inspired terror in others. He compassionately listened. He treated them as human beings. He showed them mercy. He did what they asked. He rid them of their demons. Jesus took their need seriously. Much of healing is feeling loved and understood.

Miracles vs. Nature

Some of the miracles of Jesus are not healings in the traditional sense, unless they are considered healings of the world. These miracles are events; these events are times of transformation. Nature is transformed. Nature, the universe itself, appeared to be altered by this man Jesus.

These events defy explanation or proof. They are impossible to capture in words. They are, indeed, matters of faith. They are the subject of poetry. They are the presence of God.

Christian Scripture is full of such events, as was Hebrew Scripture. These events can be understood in one of three ways:

- **As literal or physical miracles.** The world is full of events we cannot explain. The universe remains jammed with mystery. At times we must leave it at that—a mystery we cannot explain, a happening we cannot prove. We claim it as an item of faith.

- **As spiritual metaphor.** At times a story may be told whose intention is to use poetic imagery, or metaphors, to reveal a larger truth. These metaphors may not speak to a literal event or truth, but rather seek to present a deeper, more spiritual transformation.

- **As emotional events.** Emotions can transform how we see, hear, or experience an event. Emotions often have their own eyes and ears. It is true that we can at times see what we want to see or fail to see what we are too afraid to go near.

However you approach these miracle stories from Christian Scripture, they do all declare the following to be true:

- God is all-powerful.
- Jesus was sent by God.
- Faith can move mountains.
- To have faith in Jesus is to be transformed.
- To be transformed is to experience the world in a whole new way—with new eyes and ears.

A Christian believer accepts these miracles to be true. The truth may be literal or metaphoric, but to the faithful it is a gospel truth.

Jesus Calms a Storm (Matthew 8:23–27)

Jesus was crossing a lake with his disciples. A terrible storm whipped up. The disciples were terrified. Jesus was calm and had total faith—he rebuked the wind. The storm subsided.

Jesus calmed a storm. Jesus can calm our fears. Faith can rebuke the stormy winds of our lives. However you approach this miracle, it is the power of God that is revealed.

Spread the Good Word

And he said to them, "Why are you afraid, O men of little faith?" Then he rose and rebuked the wind and the sea; and there was a great calm.

—Matthew 8:26

Jesus Feeds Five Thousand (John 6:1–15)

A crowd of 5,000+ had followed Jesus. It was time for the Passover. Jesus and his disciples had only a few fish and loaves of bread. Jesus managed to feed them all—all were full. There were even leftovers.

This miracle can be approached as a sign ...

- Of the transcendent and mysterious power of God.
- Of how the great love of Jesus compelled the crowd to share the food they had brought—and most likely kept hidden, so as not to have to share.
- Of a communion-style meal, one that was tiny in size but filled the whole being.

However, you approach this sign, it remains a miracle.

Spread the Good Word

"Tell everyone to sit down," Jesus ordered. So all of them—the men alone numbered 5,000—sat down on the grassy slopes. Then Jesus took the loaves, gave thanks to God, and passed them out to the people. Afterward he did the same with the fish. And they all ate until they were full.

—John 6:10–11

Jesus Walks on Water (John 6:16–21)

The disciples were well out to sea. Again a gale swept the sea. Again the disciples were terrified. Then they saw Jesus walking across the water.

What happened here? Did Jesus walk on water? Is the message that Jesus will go to any lengths to get to us in our times of crisis? Is this story a metaphor for how faith creates a path for Jesus to come to us?

Literal truth or metaphor, the gospel truth is that God will come to us in times of need. He only asks that we dispel our fear and have faith.

Spread the Good Word

They were three or four miles out when suddenly they saw Jesus walking on the water toward the boat. They were terrified ...

—John 6:19

A Review of Miracles in Christian Scripture

It should be helpful for you to see how dominant healings and miracles are to the gospel message and to the ministry of Jesus.

They form a huge chunk of Christian Scripture. Christians are called to accept these healings and miracles as events of faith.

Ironically, it is faith alone that can comprehend them as such.

The Gospel of Matthew:

>Jesus Heals a Man with Leprosy (8:1–4)
>Jesus Heals a Roman Officer's Servant (8:5–13)
>Jesus Heals Peter's Mother-in-Law and Many Others (8:14–17)
>Jesus Calms the Storm (8:23–27)
>Jesus Heals the Man with a Legion of Demons (8:28–34)
>Jesus Heals a Paralyzed Man (9:1–8)
>Jesus Heals a Bleeding Woman and Restores a Girl to Life (9:18–26)

Jesus Heals the Blind and Mute (9:27–34)
Jesus Heals a Man's Hand on the Sabbath (12:9–14)
Jesus Feeds the 5,000 (14:13–21)
Jesus Walks on Water (14:22–33)
Jesus Heals All Who Touch Him (14:34–46)
Jesus Sends a Demon Out of a Girl (15:21–28)
Jesus Heals Many People (15:29–31)
Jesus Feeds 4,000 (15:32–39)
Jesus Heals a Demon-Possessed Boy (17:14–20)
Jesus Heals Two Blind Beggars (20:29–34)
Jesus Rises from the Dead (28:1–7)

The Gospel of Mark:

Jesus Heals Peter's Mother-in-Law and Many Others (1:29–34)
Jesus Heals a Man with Leprosy (1:40–45)
Jesus Heals a Paralyzed Man (2:1–12)
Jesus Heals a Man's Hands on the Sabbath (3:1–6)
Jesus Calms the Storm (4:35–41)
Jesus Sends Demons into a Herd of Pigs (5:1–20)
Jesus Heals a Bleeding Woman and Restores a Girl to Life (5:21–43)
Jesus Feeds 5,000 (6:30–44)
Jesus Walks on Water (6:45–52)
Jesus Heals All Who Touch Him (6:53–56)
Jesus Sends a Demon Out of a Girl (7:24–30)
Jesus Heals Many People (7:31–37)
Jesus Feeds 4,000 (8:1–10)
Jesus Restores Sight to a Blind Man (8:22–30)
Jesus Heals a Demon-Possessed Boy (9:14–29)
Jesus Heals a Blind Beggar (10:46–52)
Jesus Rises from the Dead (16:1–8)

The Gospel of Luke:

Jesus Heals Peter's Mother-in-Law and Many Others (4:38–41)
Jesus Provides a Miraculous Catch of Fish (5:1–11)
Jesus Heals a Man with Leprosy (5:12–16)
Jesus Heals a Paralyzed Man (5:17–26)

Jesus Heals a Roman Officer's Servant (7:1–10)
Jesus Raises a Widow's Son from the Dead (7:11–17)
Jesus Calms the Storm (8:22–25)
Jesus Send Demons into a Herd of Pigs (8:26–39)
Jesus Heals a Bleeding Woman and Restores a Girl to Life (8:40–56)
Jesus Heals a Demon-Possessed Boy (9:37–43)
Jesus Heals the Crippled Woman (13:10–17)
Jesus Heals a Man with Swollen Limbs (14:1–6)
Jesus Heals 10 Men with Leprosy (17:11–19)
Jesus Rises from the Dead (24:1–12)

The Gospel of John:

Jesus turns the Water into Wine (2:1–12)
Jesus Heals a Government Official's Son (4:46–54)
Jesus Heals a Lame Man by a Pool (5:1–15)
Jesus Feeds 5,000 (6:1–14)
Jesus Walks on Water (6:16–20)
Jesus Heals a Man Born Blind (9:1–2)
Jesus Raises Lazarus from the Dead (11:38–44)
Jesus Rises from the Dead (20:1–10)

The Good Word

Following many of Jesus' healings, the person healed was asked to keep the healing quiet. Jesus was aware that healings were both a catalyst for gaining followers—inspiring faith—as well as mobilizing forces against him—provoking doubt. A miracle or a healing was always controversial, even offensive, because it could only be approached from the perspective of faith.

Healings and Miracles— a Summary

Here is what we know about the nature of miracles as revealed to us in Christian Scripture:

- Healings require an absence of fear.
- Healings require the presence of faith.
- Healings often require the experience of grace—unconditional love and forgiveness.
- Healings often require mercy.
- Healings often touch those the world will not touch—the untouchable.
- Healings can remove the demons of guilt, shame, and trauma.
- Healings embrace the lost, lonely, or forgotten.
- Healings are miraculous in their power to transform the body, the heart, the soul, the spirit, or the world.
- Healings and miracles are acts of God.
- Healings and miracles display the presence and power of God.
- Jesus was a medium of that presence.
- Some miracles remain utter mysteries.
- All mystery points to the reality of a higher power.
- All mystery displays the fingerprints of God.
- Miracles are events of grace.
- Miracles are occasions for faith.
- Jesus is the event of grace.

The Least You Need to Know

- Jesus was a healer and a maker of miracles.
- Healings often require great faith and forgiveness, or deeply touching a person with love and understanding.
- Mental illness was often what people called demon possession.

- Miracles declare that Jesus is divine: He calmed storms; he walked on water; he fed 5,000 with food for 5.

- Christian Scripture points to healings and miracles as evidence that Jesus is the Christ.

Chapter 15

Jesus as Prophet: Passion Week

In This Chapter

- Jesus enters triumphantly into Jerusalem
- Jesus clears the Temple
- Jesus' authority is challenged
- Jesus shares the Last Supper with the disciples
- Jesus goes on trial and is ultimately crucified

Jesus was a prophet. A prophet plays a part. A prophet is selected by God for a significant spiritual role—to be his messenger. The whole nature of prophesy is dramatic. Prophets spoke with urgency and power. Their message was intended to stir hearts.

They sought to provoke a response. They wanted their audiences to feel, to be jarred loose. Prophets were fearless. They preached doom. They preached hope. They were larger than life.

Jesus often played the role of the prophet. His message was often prophetic. As a prophet, Jesus turned the world upside down.

As you read this chapter, you will be confronted by the powerful events of Passion Week. This chapter makes a case for why the Good News needed first to be bad news—very bad news. This chapter should help you comprehend why Christians call Good Friday "good." The events of Passion Week do not document the celebration of a hero, but the tragic demise of a prophet. Passion Week leads to one and only one place—the Cross.

His Message

Jesus told his followers:

- The last would be first and the first last.
- They must be a servant to all.
- They must be willing to wash feet.
- They must be willing to pick up their crosses and follow.
- They must risk being persecuted.
- They must risk alienating even their own family and friends.
- They must be willing to love their enemies.
- They must forgive again and again and again.
- They must turn the other cheek.
- They must touch the untouchable, seek out the lost, and befriend the outcast.
- They must follow stars.
- They must be unafraid to die for the truth.

Jesus' message and ministry were dramatic events. The fact that Jesus chose to be such a passionate prophetic voice guaranteed that his life would be filled with drama.

At no point was this choice of drama more evident than in the events of what is called Passion Week. The fact that the Passion Play is an actual international event should come as no surprise. Passion Week records the dramatic events that led to Jesus' crucifixion.

Passion Week is a play. It has several acts:

Act I	The Triumphant Entry into Jerusalem
Act II	The Clearing of the Temple
Act III	Jesus' Authority Is Challenged in the Temple
Act IV	The Last Supper
Act V	The Trial; the Epilogue—the Resurrection

The protagonist of this drama is Jesus. He plays the lead, the role of the one who has been called to deliver a message to God's people, the prophet. He delivers the message that the world will always hate the prophet.

The world will kill prophets. God alone knows the worth and value of a prophet. God alone embraces the prophetic voice. Faith in God enables us to embrace this voice as well.

Prophets call for the building of the Kingdom, a kingdom quite unlike the world, a kingdom built with justice, mercy, and equality. The Kingdom becomes the set of the Passion Week play.

The Kingdom is used to determine the makeup and costumes of all characters. The Kingdom even dictates the lights and sound system used.

Let the play begin. The curtain rises. We begin to see the Kingdom appear from out of a morning mist.

The Triumphant Entry to Jerusalem (Luke 19:28–44)

Every Palm Sunday I am full of fear. All the little kids are given palms to carry, and the palms make a nifty sword. Within minutes, no matter how thoroughly we caution them, the kids are playing pirate, and huge sword fights ensue. I try very hard to get the kids to understand the true meaning of Palm Sunday, but it isn't easy. Most of the kids will always think of Palm Sunday as sword-fighting Sunday.

Palm Sunday is the beginning of Passion Week. It marks the triumphal entry of Jesus into Jerusalem. Scripture tells us that Jesus' arrival was greeted by the strewing of palms before him.

This entire event was staged by Jesus. It was a carefully planned piece of prophetic theater. I see it as a liturgical drama. Each and every moment of Jesus' arrival had been mapped out, more important, it had been prayerfully and spiritually thought out as well.

Here is what happened and why it was staged in this manner:

- Jesus and his disciples came to the towns of Bethphage and Bethany.

- Jesus sent two disciples ahead. He instructed them to look for a young colt that had never been ridden—a donkey.

- Jesus knew this colt would be waiting for them.

- Jesus told them to tell the owner of the colt that the Lord was in need of it, which was exactly what happened.

- By this time Jesus was well known.

- It was Passover time in Jerusalem, and the city was jammed with people.

- Jesus wanted a large audience for this drama.

- As he came down the road from the Mount of Olives, his followers began to sing his praises and to lay palm branches before him.

- Zechariah 9:9 says, "Look, your king is coming to you. He is righteous and victorious, yet he is humble, riding on a donkey—even on a donkey's colt."

- Jesus arrived on a donkey's colt, fulfilling prophesy and heralding his coming as the Messiah.

- Jesus was a gifted student of the prophets.

- Jesus knew exactly what he was doing in arriving on the back of a donkey's colt.

- The Pharisees, or religious establishment, were furious with Jesus for staging such a spectacle.

- The Pharisees asked for the crowds to be dispersed.

- Jesus told the Pharisees that even if the crowds were quiet, the stones would shout.

- Jesus wept over Jerusalem. He anticipated the rejection to come.

- The people were looking for a Messiah who would be a great nationalistic king. Soon disappointed, many in the crowd would turn on Jesus.

Jesus Clears the Temple (Mark 11:15–19)

Jesus was a man. He fully embraced being a human being. He had a temper. He was noticeably enraged by seeing injustice. Whenever he witnessed people using or abusing other people, his temper would flare. This was most true when he felt people were abusing folks who were seeking God.

Money-changers and merchants did big business during Passover. Foreigners were forced to have their money changed into Temple currency. The Temple tax had to be paid with a particular coinage. The money changers used an inflated rate of exchange and made a bundle off these spiritual pilgrims. The doves that were used in ritual Temple sacrifices were also being sold at an exorbitant price.

The Good Word

This act of the play is devoted to Jesus' cleansing the Temple. It displays an angry Jesus preparing the Temple for true worship and enabling the Gentiles to worship as well. Jesus drove out the forces of greed and injustice. He swept the Temple clean of sin. This act also fulfills prophesy. In Isaiah 56:7, Isaiah states, "I will accept their burnt offerings and sacrifices, because my Temple will be called a house of prayer for all nations." The Temple was now ready for genuine worship and prayer.

Jesus was livid to see the Temple being turned into a den of robbers. Jesus drove the merchants from their stalls in the Temple Court of the Gentiles. These stalls occupied most of the space in the court-yard and actually kept Gentiles from being able to worship God. This, too, infuriated Jesus.

The Temple had become similar to an airport. When you are at an airport, you are trapped. You have to pay exorbitant prices for food or merchandise, especially souvenirs, because you have no place else to go. You don't want to miss your plane. The Temple pilgrims did not wish to miss their opportunity to worship at Temple during the sacred Passover.

Jesus' Authority Is Challenged (Mark 11:27–33)

The religious leaders asked Jesus who gave him the authority to drive out the money-changers and merchants. This was clearly a trap. The dramatic tension of the play is rising. Jesus knew he would be confronted.

If Jesus answered that his authority came from God, they would ac-cuse him of blasphemy. If he said he acted on his own authority, they would brand him a nut. Jesus was wise enough to counter a question with a question. He asked them if John's baptism was a heavenly event or merely an earthly one. The Pharisees knew that many people believed John the Baptist to be a prophet, so because they feared a riot, they dropped this line of questioning.

The Pharisees despised Jesus. He exposed the shallowness of their faith and their hypocrisy. He undermined their authority.

He was eroding their stature and power.

Jesus Faces More Stiff Questioning by the Pharisees (Mark 12:13–34)

The Pharisees continued to question Jesus every chance they got:

- They questioned him about paying taxes. (Mark 12:13–17)
- They questioned him about the Resurrection. (Mark 12:18–27)
- They questioned him about the Greatest Commandment. (Mark 12:28–34)

All these periods of questioning were no more than traps set by the Pharisees. They wanted to give themselves reason for ridding themselves of Jesus. They wanted to prove Jesus a fraud.

Jesus Warns Against the Religious Establishment (Mark 12:38–40)

Jesus was scathing in his attack on the Pharisees. He called them pure phonies. He stated that their religion was all show with no substance. He also accused them of cheating widows. No long public prayers could cover up their greed or their shameless behavior. They would be punished eternally. The Pharisees are the villains of this drama.

The Olivet Discourse (Mark 13)

Here Jesus talked about both the End Times (Mark 13:1–23), and the Second Coming (Mark 13:24–27). This entire discourse is delivered as prophesy. Jesus did not put his predictions in any chronological order; he simply encouraged his followers to be prepared for his return. If we are busy following him now, we will be busy following him when he returns.

Again, Jesus was building the wall between himself and the religious establishment. The plot of the play is thickening. The dramatic tension mounts.

The Olivet Discourse is also loaded with references from the prophets of Hebrew Scripture—in particular Daniel (please note Daniel 9:26–27 and 7:13–14).

The Last Supper (Mark 14:17–31)

Jesus used every scene of this drama to directly challenge the religious establishment. He mocked their faith. He met their questions with questions of scorn. He gave them more and more reason to hate him.

Jesus came to Jerusalem to declare that he was the Messiah. There was no backing away from that message. Jesus knew that the

Pharisees would ask for the death of anyone making such an outrageous claim. Jesus embraced being outrageous and offensive.

He drove fully into his prophetic role in this Passion Week play.

The Last Supper was another staged event. It was Jesus' way of making it official—the end was near. Jesus gathered his disciples together one last time. They ate a meal, sang some psalms, and shared Scripture. At this point Jesus took the traditional parts of the Passover meal, the passing of bread and the drinking of wine, and gave them a whole new meaning. His words to his disciples celebrated closure. His act of sharing bread and wine, symbolic of his own body and blood, dramatically declared that the cross was on the horizon.

The Good Word

It was during the Last Supper that Jesus also prophetically announced that Judas would betray him and Peter would deny him.

The Upper Room (John 13–17)

The Gospel of John offers a unique perspective on how Jesus prepared his disciples for his departure. In John 13–17 we hear Jesus speaking directly to his disciples about what they can expect after he is gone. He makes it clear that he must go, and equally clear that he had prepared them well to handle his departure. He would leave them with the gift of his Holy Spirit. They would not be alone.

Jesus worked hard on saying good-bye. He truly put forth every effort to spiritually ready his disciples for his death. Jesus was remarkably courageous as he approached the cross.

The Garden of Gethsemane (Mark 14:32–42)

Jesus was human. He struggled mightily with his impending death. He prayed for God to find another path for him to take. Seeing no way out, Jesus prayerfully accepted his fate—the will of God.

Jesus was deeply wounded by his disciples. While he agonized over what awaited him, they were fast asleep. In the end, the disciples proved unable to deal with the reality of the cross. They functioned as if the ministry would somehow be restored and Jesus would somehow be saved. Jesus was simply unable to convince them that he knew not only the will of the Pharisees but the will of God as well. And he also knew his friends. They would betray, deny, and abandon him.

Jesus Betrayed and Arrested (Mark 14:43–52)

The drama is marching toward its conclusion. The cast of characters play their roles to perfection. Judas betrayed Jesus, just as predicted. Ironically, and tragically, Judas betrayed Jesus with a kiss. Jesus was arrested. The disciples deserted him.

The Trial

The trial of Jesus was staged in six powerful scenes. The trial probably lasted less than 18 hours, but included 6 different hearings:

- **The hearing before Annas (John 18:12–24).** Annas was still viewed as the High Priest by the Jews, in spite of the fact that the Romans had chosen another person in his place.

- **The hearing before Caiaphas (Matthew 26:57–68).** This hearing was held at night and in secrecy. Caiaphas was the High Priest. The trial is a mockery of justice. Guilt is declared without evidence.

- **The trial before the high council (Matthew 27:1–2).** Seventy members of the high council met to rubber-stamp the results of the two previous hearings.

- **The first hearing before Pilate (Luke 23:1–5).** Jesus is charged with treason and rebellion before the Roman governor. Pilate knew Jesus was innocent but feared the uproar of the Pharisees.

- **The hearing before Herod (Luke 23:6–12).** Pilate sent Jesus to Herod Antipas, the ruler of Galilee, Jesus' home. Herod returned him to Pilate, disappointed that Jesus failed to perform a miracle.

- **The last hearing before Pilate (Luke 23:13–25).** Another uprising in his district and Pilate would get the boot. He relented and handed Jesus over for execution.

The irony of these hearings was that nothing was heard. Nobody was interested in hearing anything Jesus had to say. They simply needed to go through the motions. Their ears, like their minds, were shut.

The Crucifixion (Mark 15:20–41)

Death on a cross is unimaginable agony. Jesus died a brutal death. His family and friends must have been traumatized. Prisoners were forced to carry their own crosses. Jesus was so weakened by the beatings ordered by Pilate that he was unable to carry his cross the whole way. A bystander, Simon the Cyrene, a foreign visitor there for the Passover, was made to carry Jesus' cross to Golgotha—"Skull Hill."

The final speech of the Passion Week play is not so much an oration, as it is a collection of short sayings—the Seven Last Words:

Jesus was wholly forgiving:

> Father forgive these people because they don't know what they are doing.
>
> —Luke 23:34

Jesus offered hope to the criminal at his side:

> I assure you, today you will be with me in paradise.
>
> —Luke 23:43

Jesus embraced his beloved mother Mary and disciple John with his wish for their healing and happiness:

> Woman, he is your son ... She is your mother.
>
> —John 19:26–27

Jesus was fully human. He shouted his doubt angrily at God:

> My God, my God, why have you forsaken me?
>
> —Matthew 27:46, Mark 15:34

Jesus was human. He had a real body. He knew real agony on the cross:

> I am thirsty.
>
> —John 19:28

Jesus knew his death was imminent. His ministry completed. His message sealed:

> It is finished.
>
> —John 19:30

Jesus displayed divine faith:

> Father, I entrust my spirit into your hands!
>
> —Luke 23–46

The Good Word

Christians are called to know why they call Good Friday good. Why do Christians celebrate the crucifixion as an event of goodness?

Because, as a Christian, I am aware that the world ultimately rejects the grace of God. Jesus, the event of grace, could not be claimed by the wisdom of the world. Only faith can grasp the goodness of Jesus. Only faith can comprehend the victory declared by Christ's death. Only faith can bear witness to why loss is the soil in which hope blooms.

The Least You Need to Know

- Palm Sunday—Jesus arrived triumphantly in Jerusalem.
- Jesus fulfilled prophesy and declared that he was the Messiah by arriving on the back of a donkey's colt.

- Jesus drove out the money-changers and merchants from the Temple.

- Jesus' authority and credibility were incessantly questioned by the religious leaders.

- Maundy Thursday—Jesus gathered the disciples for a last meal and the celebration of the first communion.

- Good Friday—Jesus was betrayed, arrested, put on trial for treason, and ultimately crucified.

Part 6

Christian Scripture: Jesus as the Christ

Did Jesus rise from the dead? The Bible is clear that several people witnessed the risen Christ:

- *Mary Magdalene—Mark 16:9–11*
- *The women at the tomb—Matthew 28:8–10*
- *Peter in Jerusalem—Luke 24:34*
- *The two travelers on the road—Mark 16:12–13*
- *Ten disciples behind closed doors—John 20:19–25*
- *Seven disciples while fishing—John 21:1–14*
- *Eleven disciples on the mountain—Matthew 28:16–20*
- *All the disciples except Judas—John 20:26–31*

These appearances are seen as crucial evidence that Jesus continues to live and reign in the lives of believers.

Believers take a leap of faith. They have faith in what they cannot see. They have faith in what they cannot touch. They leap to a place where they believe Jesus can be found. They find on the other side a Jesus who welcomes them with abundant grace. Flying in faith over a chasm of doubt, they locate a vitally present and powerful Christ, ready and willing to transform their lives. The risen Jesus declares that Jesus is the Christ, the eternal Lord.

Chapter 16

Opening Paul's Mail

In This Chapter

- Paul's profile
- Paul's Gospel
- Paul and the shaping of the Church
- Paul's mail

Paul. Paul the apostle. In the history of Christianity, nobody except Jesus was of greater importance. Paul was born in Tarsus and raised a Jew. He was trained to be a Pharisee. His training probably included tutelage by Gamaliel. Paul became fully devoted to his religion and the Law that anchored it.

Paul knew Hebrew Scripture. He also knew of Jesus and the people who followed him—people of The Way. He saw this Christian movement as a grave threat to Judaism. He became rabid in his hatred for people of The Way. He even came to persecute Christians.

Paul eventually traveled to Damascus. His sole purpose was to capture Christians and bring them back to Jerusalem. It was on the road to Damascus that Paul had a dramatic conversion experience. It can be said that Paul met Jesus Christ on that road.

Paul's life was turned completely around. He was headed one way and then suddenly he was moving in the opposite direction. Paul the persecutor of Christians became Paul the converter of Christians. Paul became the key to spreading the gospel to non-Jews. Paul worked with Barnabas in Antioch and eventually made three missionary journeys across the Roman Empire.

As you read this chapter, the person and faith of Paul will come to life for you. You will learn a good deal about his version of events—Paul's very own gospel message. You will come to see why he is such a vital figure in the formation of the early church. His letters will reveal to you his passionate struggle to keep the church true to its calling—serving Jesus Christ.

Paul—Born Again?

I think of Paul as one of the first born-again Christians. Paul had a dramatic encounter with the risen Christ and was totally transformed by the event. He felt brand-new. He saw the world in a whole new way. Jesus had become the center of his existence. Paul was born again. Now, in many respects this was a good thing for Paul, but it also had its drawbacks.

On the positive side:

- Paul had found acceptance and love in his experience of Christ.
- Paul had a fresh and passionate faith in the risen Lord.
- Paul felt a personal relationship to Jesus.
- Paul was no longer filled with hate but with grace.
- Paul would no longer need to persecute Christians or anyone else.

On the negative side:

- Paul's beliefs could be black and white, inflexible, even judgmental.
- Paul could be a know-it-all—arrogant, self-righteous, and rude.
- Paul was prone to trying to ram his faith down other people's throats.

- Paul was easily irritated and had a tough time keeping his anger under control.

- Once a fanatic, to some degree, always a fanatic.

It is always difficult for a new convert to present his faith with graciousness and maturity. At times we need to be confronted with such passionate urgency, but faith is best expressed with respect for the other person's perspective.

Paul's Ministry

Paul's letters to various churches become a major portion of the Christian Scripture. These letters speak to the spiritual issues of individuals and the church, as well as addressing some of the thorniest religious issues of his time.

Paul worked diligently on behalf of non-Jews. He sought to convince Jews that non-Jews were acceptable, even if they did not obey all of the Jewish laws. Paul spent most of his ministry trying to convince non-Jews that though they were not Jews, they were acceptable in the eyes of Christ. Paul was the apostle to the Gentiles.

Paul was an evangelist. His task was to spread the good news of Jesus Christ and to win converts to a fledgling church. In most respects, Paul was totally unsuited to the task. He is described in the acts of Paul and Thecla as being bald and bowlegged, short and squat, with eyebrows that converged over a bulbous nose. In other words, Paul was no TV evangelist.

Paul was also quite sickly. He speaks often of a "thorn in the flesh," which may have been epilepsy or even mental illness.

His personality was intense. He was a nonstop talker. He was always trying to win over some convert. He must have coaxed and bullied his listeners. The fact is that Paul was not charismatic. There was not much about Paul that would have drawn you to him. Quite the opposite. He sounds like a human pit bull—we'd probably want to run away.

Paul's ministry was compelled by what he experienced on the road to Damascus (Acts 9:1–6, 22:4–16, 26:9–18). He was compulsive in his ministry. He was driven. After meeting Jesus, he no longer felt in the driver's seat of his life. Jesus was now the chauffeur, and he merely the appreciative passenger. Paul's road experience had given him a lifelong lump in the throat. It was this same lump that he tried to pass on to Gentiles all over the Roman Empire.

Paul traveled far and wide to spread the Good News. He went to Corinth, Ephesus, Thessalonica, Galatia, and Collossae. He also ventured to Jerusalem, Cyprus, Crete, Malta, Athens, Syracuse, and Rome. This was like a whistle-stop campaign trip—Jesus for Messiah. He virtually hit every important stop in the Mediterranean world.

Paul planted churches. He really did. He planted the seeds of faith among those he believed would garden. His letters were attempts to give these gardeners tips on how to keep the soil fertile, the plants watered, and the garden free of weeds and pests.

Paul's Gospel

As Paul traveled, he shared the Good News of Jesus Christ. But it was Paul's version. Paul had a unique perspective on faith and on what was essential to living the Christian life. Paul's vantage point was heavily influenced by his background and conversion experience. The following sections express the five major themes of Paul's Gospel.

The Grace of God

Paul had done nothing to win the Lord's favor. In fact, his persecution of Christians must have dramatically displeased his Lord. Paul's conversion came as a shock of acceptance, affirmation, and approval. Paul had never before known such unconditional love. Paul became a strong advocate of the belief that it is by grace alone that we are saved—in Paul's case, saved from himself.

> God saved you by his special favor when you believed. And you can't take credit for this; it is a gift from God. Salvation is not a reward for the good things we have done, so none of us can boast about it. For we are God's masterpiece. He has created us anew in Christ Jesus, so that we can do the good things he planned for us long ago.
>
> —Ephesians 2:8–10

The Law

Though Paul had a deep and abiding respect for the Law, he acknowledged the sin of perfectionism that it incited. Trying to keep the Law in all its detail kept Paul from being a loving or merciful human being. It was his fierce devotion to the Law that created Paul the persecutor. The Law was nothing more than an attempt by human beings to play God. By trying to be religiously perfect, they ultimately saw themselves as on par with God.

> The law of Moses could not save us, because of our sinful nature. But God put into effect a different plan to save us. He sent his own Son in a human body like ours, except that ours are sinful. God destroyed sin's control over us by giving his Son as a sacrifice for our sins.
>
> —Romans 8:3

Fools for Christ

Paul knew how foolish the gospel must have sounded to Jewish ears, even to Gentile ears: the idea of a crucified Messiah, of a Kingdom that was not about power or prestige, of a faith that does not appear to guarantee blessings and a pain-free existence. What fool would follow this Jesus?

> I know very well how foolish the message of the cross sounds to those who are on the road to destruction. But we who are being saved recognize this message as the very power of God.
>
> —1 Corinthians 1:18

Christ Who Lives in Me

Paul knew all about human limitations. He knew that human beings were prone to judgment, jealousy, envy, and disdain for other human beings. He knew how petty people could be. He knew how easily humanity could find reason to hate.

He also knew that Jesus could be worn like a cloak. He encouraged his listeners to put Jesus on. To wear him. To act as if they were Christ. To see each other through Christ's eyes.

> I myself no longer live, but Christ lives in me.
>
> —Galatians 2:20

The Life in the Spirit

Paul asked us to *be* the virgin Mary. He asked that Jesus be born in us. The spiritual life is how we both receive the presence of Christ as well as how we give that presence back to the world. The spiritual life is maturation.

The spiritual life is for adults only. The life in the spirit is the pursuit of holiness in all that we say and do. The spiritual life is to become a living sacrifice for the Lord.

Paul commanded us to live as God's beloved children. He demanded that we be instruments of God's grace. He called us to be the living presence of the love of God.

The Good Word

Paul's Gospel is quite lean and simple. We are saved by the grace of God. Because we are saved, we choose to lead spiritual lives. Spirituality is the choice to celebrate being human, maturation, and the chance to become holy. Our goal as Christians is to literally become Christ.

Paul and the Church

Paul was like a parent to the early church. He had sought to offer them encouragement, guidance, love, and discipline. His letters were earnest attempts to keep in touch. A parent may say good-bye to her offspring, letting them fly from the nest, but once a parent always a parent. Paul always wanted to be a part of the lives of these churches.

Paul's letters were parental in tone and content. Let me review some of the key points made in several of Paul's epistles to the early church.

- **The Church in Rome (Romans).** Paul focused the church in Rome on faith. It was their faith alone that had saved them from sin. Justified by faith, Christians are called to sanctification. Sanctifying means to *make holy*. Christians are commissioned to lead holy lives. It was in Roman that Christians were called to be living sacrifices. (Romans 12:1–2)

- **The Church in Corinth (Corinthians 1 and 2).** Paul first addressed a schism he saw growing in this church: Their loyalties were being divided between Peter, Paul, and Apollos. He also spoke to a moral laxity in terms of sexuality. Paul spoke to a lack of order in worship, namely people taking the Lord's supper without first confessing their sins.

This first letter addressed a church that has fallen into disunity and disorder. Paul sought to correct abuses. He offered a Christian solution to each issue. He also preached a message of *freedom*. Christian freedom does not grant permission to treat others in a mean-spirited way.

Freedom = obedience

We are free to obey. If we obey, we love. If we love, we serve Christ. Love was the only way available to solve the divisions in this church.

Spread the Good Word

There are three things that will endure—faith, hope, and love—and the greatest of these is love.

—1 Corinthians 13:13

Paul's second letter to the church in Corinth was defensive. He was defending himself and his authority. Paul was being challenged by false teachers. Paul was asking the church to remain true to the Christian doctrine he had taught them. Paul was warning the church against false teachers. Paul was alarmed by pagan influences upon the church.

Paul also encouraged giving to the needy. Paul organized a fund for the poor in the Jerusalem church and encouraged the church in Corinth to be true to its stewardship commitments and to be generous to those in need.

- **The Church in Galatia (Galatians).** A group of Jewish leaders were seeking to impose Jewish law upon non-Jews. These Jewish Christians believed that you must follow the law of Moses, be circumcised, and have faith in Jesus Christ. Paul was in opposition. He taught again that the Law could not save a soul. Paul admonished the church in Galatia not to fall back into legalism. He told them that their faith had set them free. They were free from the endless shame and guilt necessitated by strict adherence to the Law. Paul advocated for a Holy Spirit which would enable them to lead a new life, one of joy, peace, and a true celebration of the equality of all believers.

- **The Church in Ephesus (Ephesians).** Paul preached in this letter. He told the church that God alone was the center of the universe and the author of all history. He described the church as a living body and that each part of the body had a unique and vital role to fill. This was a letter that asked the church to have no excuses for having divisions. There is no excuse for discrimination of any kind. The Holy Spirit will keep us unified, grounded in grace, ruled by love.

Spread the Good Word

We are all one body, we have the same Spirit, and we have all been called to the same glorious future. There is only one Lord, one faith, one baptism, and there is only one God and Father, who is over us all and in us all and living through us all.

—Ephesians 4:4–6

- **The Church at Philippi (Philippians).** This letter was written from prison. Paul suffered greatly for his message and ministry. Ironically, this letter is about joy. Paul told the believers in Philippi that joy comes from service, sacrifice, and even suffering. Here again, Paul's Gospel sounded foolish to the world.

- **The Church in Colosse (Colossians).** Paul again wrote from prison. Paul had never actually visited this church. Paul sought here to battle the syncretism that infiltrated the church.

He especially focused on the Gnostic heresy, which emphasized a special knowledge (Gnosis in Greek) and denied Jesus as God and Savior. Paul was clear: Jesus is the leader of the church; Jesus is God; Jesus Christ requires first place in all of our lives.

All of Paul's letters are human and personal. I doubt they were ever intended to be seen in print. They are filled with grammatical errors as well as rushes of human irritation and judgment.

Paul wrote as a parent. He wrote with love. He wrote with hurt, anger, and fear. He wrote as someone who believes his children must be on their own but that he alone knows how to take proper care of them.

These letters are wonderfully and powerfully real. They speak of real faith, real issues within the church, real feelings, and the real importance of Paul in the life of the early church. As letters, they make for difficult Scripture. Full of humanness. Full of seeming contradictions. Full of feeling. As letters, they also make for profound pieces of Scripture, because they are so clearly motivated by a passionate faith in the risen Lord.

Paul's Top Ten

I think it might be helpful here to list what I consider Paul's top 10 beliefs. These beliefs can be seen in some, several, or all of his letters. This top 10 offers you a good summary of the contents of Paul's mail.

- We are justified by faith alone.
- We are saved by grace.

- Grace calls us to holy lives.
- The Holy Spirit will teach us how to live holy lives.
- The spiritual life includes suffering, service, and sacrifice.
- The spiritual life is for adults only, as only adults can fulfill Christ's call to lives of love and forgiveness. Only an adult can know the hope and joy that comes from being obedient to the Lord.
- The church must celebrate and discipline the spiritual life.
- The church must celebrate the diversity of gifts found in the faithful.
- The church must, at all times, be unified by faith in Jesus Christ.
- There is one God. One faith. One baptism. One church.

Paul was true to his calling to convert Gentiles to faith in Christ. He was a major force in the building of the early church. His Gospel continues to influence Christianity in today's world.

The Least You Need to Know

- Paul was the Apostle to the Gentiles.
- Paul was an evangelist and missionary.
- Paul preached and taught a message of grace over Law.
- Paul was crucial in the establishment of several churches.
- Paul's letters admonished the church to be unified in faith.
- Paul letters addressed many religious squabbles within the early church.

Chapter 17

The Disciples Act Up and Out (Acts)

In This Chapter

- Pentecost and Peter's sermon
- Stephen's martyrdom
- Peter and Paul, brothers and rivals in the faith
- James, Jesus' brother, and the Jewish-Gentile controversy
- Paul's imprisonment

The Book of Acts was written by Luke. It is the sequel to his Gospel. Since the world had not ended as most people had believed it would, Luke addressed the question, "Well, what do we do now?" What they did now was to build the church. Acts is an accurate historical record of the early church.

Acts is also a Gospel of a kind. It opens with a baptism by fire. Peter gives his version of the Sermon on the Mount. There are miracle stories. There are conversion accounts. Stephen becomes the first martyr of the early church. Peter and Paul face persecution and imprisonment for spreading the gospel.

Like the earlier life of Jesus, Peter and Paul faced stern opposition from the religious establishment. Peter and Paul preach, teach, heal, and prophesize.

As you read this chapter, you will take a good look at the Book of Acts. You will learn of the significant events that shaped and formed the early church; the Pentecost; the martyrdom of Stephen; the rivalry between Peter and Paul; the diplomatic role of James, the brother of Jesus; and the many squabbles and struggles that dominated those first years. You will also discover that the beginning of the early church was fraught with danger. Many of the leaders of the early church spent considerable time in prison.

The Book of Acts

The Book of Acts is a testimony of faith. It speaks to the power of the Holy Spirit to inspire, guide, and direct lives. It offers insights on the meaning of grace. It builds a case to defend Jesus' claim to be Lord and Savior. The Book of Acts is a gospel blend of history and faith.

The Book of Acts is an eyewitness account to the birth and the spread of the church. A small group of disciples had formed a church in Jerusalem. From there the message spread throughout the Roman Empire. The Holy Spirit was held responsible for this evangelism. The gospel was preached all the way to Rome.

The Book of Acts begins with a brief summary of Jesus' last days on Earth. This is done as a foreshadowing of the persecution many would face in the building of the Church. Luke, the author of Acts, also addressed the ascension of Jesus as well as the selection of a replacement for Judas Iscariot. Luke then moved to the point of the Book of Acts, the spread of the good news of the gospel, as well as the rapid growth of the young church.

Pentecost (Acts 2:1–13)

Pentecost is one of the most spiritually significant events in the life of the early church. Held 50 days after Passover, Pentecost celebrates the Festival of the Harvest. Jesus was crucified during the time of Passover, and now a spiritual harvest of new believers was to take place.

Pentecost also marks the day when John the Baptist's words (Luke 3:16) are fulfilled—a baptism by fire. We hear of tongues of fire. In Scripture, fire was symbolic of purification. Pentecost signals a time when peoples' hearts were ignited and the flames of faith are ablaze. The crowd that gathered to share in Pentecost was inspired by the presence of the Holy Spirit. The Holy Spirit swept over them with great wind and fire.

The Good Word

It is impossible to say just what happened at Pentecost. There was a crowd of seekers, a gathering of those looking for the presence of God, a crowd of faithful gathered to celebrate thanksgiving for the harvest, a crowd of religious revelers. This crowd was met by violent winds and fire. They spoke in tongues. They were overwhelmed by the experience. They were swept up by the Spirit. They were transformed.

All we do know for sure, is that whatever happened, it apparently happened to them all. It was powerful. It would prove unforgettable. It became a turning point in the life of the early church.

For Luke, Pentecost marked the true beginning of the Church. It was on this day that the risen Christ made himself so abundantly present that there could be no denying that his Church would be established. Pentecost was the confirmation that people from all over the world would come to know Jesus as Lord. Pentecost was the inauguration of the Holy Spirit's active presence in the shaping and forming of the early Church.

Peter—Part One (Acts 1–5)

The disciple Peter was the leader of the church in Jerusalem. He was present at Pentecost and delivered a powerful sermon following the fiery events. His sermon (Acts 2:14–42) told the crowd that Jesus is the fulfillment of Hebrew prophesy. He quoted from Joel 2:28–32 to make his point. He preached that Jesus is the Messiah. He spoke to them candidly of how the risen Christ could transform their lives. This sermon made Peter's case—Jesus is Lord and Savior.

Peter's life closely follows Jesus' footsteps, and Acts records the following events:

- Peter healed a crippled beggar. (3:1–11)
- Peter preached in the Temple. (3:12–26)
- Peter and John were confronted by the Sadducees. The Sadducees did not believe in the resurrection; Peter and John were arrested; Peter spoke boldly of the risen Christ. (4:1–22)
- Ananias and Sapphira committed a sin against the Holy Spirit. They sold land and told the apostles they would receive all the money, yet they gave them only a portion. Peter confronted their greed and deceit. (5:1–11)
- The apostles healed many people. (5:12–16)
- The apostles met stiff opposition from the Sanhedrin. The 70 men of the High Council wanted to rid themselves of this nuisance. (5:17–32)
- Gamaliel, a popular Pharisee, convinced the High Council to let the apostles go. (5:33–42)

As you can see, Peter's ministry was full of controversy and suffering, imprisonment, beatings, corruption, and deceit. The early church faced huge obstacles in spreading the good news.

Stephen (Acts 6–7)

The 12 disciples (the original 11 plus Matthias, who replaced Judas) were plagued by the problem of meeting the needs of the people. The distribution of food to the poor became an area of conflict.

The Christians who spoke Greek felt they were being discriminated against in favor of the native Jewish Christians who spoke Hebrew.

In an effort to correct this problem, the apostles named seven deacons. These deacons were all Greek-speaking. The seven deacons were Stephen, Philip, Procorus, Nicanor, Timon, Parmenas, and Nicolas of Antioch. These men were chosen as ministers, and their ministry was one of compassion. They were to be the hands of Christ feeding the poor, binding the brokenhearted, and proclaiming the acceptable year of the Lord.

Stephen was well known for his faith. He was seen as a man of great wisdom, grace, honesty, and character. He was a man of integrity.

A group of Jewish slaves who had been freed by Rome and who had formed a synagogue in Jerusalem lied about Stephen, saying that he spoke against the Law of Moses. Stephen was arrested and brought before the High Council. The Sadducees, the dominant party on the Council, were devoted to the Law of Moses. The accusations Stephen faced before the Council were exactly those that Jesus had faced. (Matthew 26:59–61) Stephen was up against Caiaphas, the same man who had earlier questioned and condemned Jesus.

Though Stephen proved himself to be a man of formidable faith and debating skills, as well as a keen student of the Law of Moses, he was stoned to death while pleading for forgiveness for his persecutors. Stephen's life was a spiritual cloning of that of Jesus.

Spread the Good Word

And as they stoned him, Stephen prayed, "Lord Jesus, receive my spirit." And he fell to his knees shouting, "Lord, don't charge them with this sin!" And with that, he died.

—Acts 7:59–60

Philip (Acts 6:1–7, 8:5–40, 21:8–10)

Philip was a deacon, one of the seven selected to distribute food to the needy. He was forced to leave Jerusalem due to the increased persecution. Ironically, Paul was one of those leading this persecution.

Philip thus became a missionary and traveled to Samaria. As you might recall, Samaritans were despised by the Jews and were the victims of terrible prejudice.

It is no coincidence that Philip chose to evangelize in Samaria. Philip was an enormous success. Peter and John joined him there. In a strange desert encounter with an Ethiopian *eunuch*, Philip managed to bring this foreigner to faith in Christ. This meeting is used to symbolize Philip's belief that the gospel is universal and available to all.

> ### Password
> A **eunuch** is a person without any sexual organs.

Philip eventually came to Caesarea, where he later became host to Paul—ironically, one of those who originally forced him to flee Jerusalem.

Peter—Part Two (Acts 9–12)

The church was beginning to thrive. Philip had had great success in Samaria, and Peter was successful in his preaching in Judea and Galilee. Peter healed Aeneas in Lydda and Dorcas in Joppa. (Acts 9:31–43) These healings were experienced as signs of the ongoing presence of the Holy Spirit in Peter's ministry.

It was while in Joppa that Peter had a vision. This vision told him that he could and must evangelize to the Gentiles. Peter shared the gospel message with Cornelius, and his entire household became believers. The church in Jerusalem was surprisingly supportive of

Peter's efforts to minister to Gentiles. The message was next taken to Antioch, where Barnanbas had been trying to win converts.

Herod joined in the persecution of the Jerusalem church. Herod had James, Jesus' brother, killed, and he imprisoned Peter. Peter had a miraculous escape from prison. He walked to a prayer meeting being held on his behalf at the home of Mary, the mother of John Mark. John Mark was a missionary intern and a supposed Gospel writer. He was a companion to Peter, Paul, and Barnabas on their missionary journeys.

Spread the Good Word

The eunuch asked Philip, "Was Isaiah talking about himself or someone else?" So Philip began with this same Scripture and then used many others to tell him the Good News about Jesus.

—Acts 8:34—35

Paul (Acts 13:1–28:31)

Paul's ministry dominates the second half of Acts. Paul and Barnabsas took the gospel message to Cyprus and Galatia, where they experienced tremendous success, though the dispute over the evangelism of the Gentiles continued to haunt their ministry.

The fact that large numbers of Gentiles were coming to faith in Christ was posing a major threat for the church as a whole. A council was held in Jerusalem to deal with this dispute. The primary focus of the council was to determine how Gentiles should deal with the Jewish laws. It was James, Jesus' brother, who managed to reach a compromise solution.

After the council, Paul and Silas preached in Antioch. They then embarked upon a journey to Syria and Cilicia. At this same time, Barnabas and Mark were headed off to evangelize Cyprus. This was

Paul's second missionary journey. He would establish churches in Philippi, Thessalonica, Berea, Corinth, and Ephesus. He then returned to Antioch.

Paul's third missionary adventure took him through Galatia, Phrygia, Macedonia, and Achaia. It was during this pilgrimage that Paul felt compelled to return to Jerusalem. He was warned not to return, but chose to go.

While in Jerusalem, Paul was assaulted by an angry mob and taken into protective custody by a Roman commander. Paul was put on trial before the Jewish High Council, as well as Felix, the governor, and Augustus and Agrippa. Paul's defense of his faith was firm and fervent. He appealed to Caesar, and his case was sent to Rome.

As he sailed to Rome, the ship was swamped by a nasty storm. The sailors and prisoners were forced to swim for shore. Heroically, Paul used this occasion to once again plead his case, that Jesus was the Messiah, the event of grace, the living Lord. Acts closes with Paul still at it. He was preaching and teaching in prison, still trying to win converts to Christ.

The Cast and Crew

In the drama recorded in Acts, Peter and Paul played the leads. Stephen and Philip were the supporting players, along with Barnabas, Silas, and John Mark. There was, however, a major crew that worked behind the scenes. This crew brought the production to life.

- **The Crippled Man.** He was healed by Peter and praised God. (3:9–12)
- **Cornelius.** He was able to demonstrate to Peter that the gospel was also for Gentiles. (10:30–35)
- **Rhoda.** She convinced Paul to find safety in Mary's home. (12:13–15)
- **James.** Jesus' brother and a spiritual diplomat, he led the Jerusalem Council with wisdom and grace. (15:13–21)
- **Lydia.** She opened her home to Paul and became the foundation of the church in Philippi. (16:13–15)

- **Jason.** He allowed Paul to stay in his home and risked his life on behalf of what he believed. (17:5–9)
- **Julius.** He spared Paul; other soldiers wanted to kill him. (27:1, 43)

The Gospel of Acts

Acts preaches and teaches a gospel all its own. It is a spiritual cloning of the other Gospels, a recasting of the story in the lives of the leaders of the early church. Here is a summation of what I consider the core gospel message of the Book of Acts:

- Jesus Christ lives.
- Jesus Christ is embodied in the Holy Spirit.
- The Holy Spirit infuses disciples and new believers with the courage needed to face incessant persecution.
- The religious establishment, represented by the Jewish Law, will work hard to destroy the new church.
- A tested faith is a strong faith.
- The faithful will be martyred.
- The gospel message cannot be stopped.
- The gospel message is universal.
- Jesus is the Christ for all believers, Jewish or Gentile.
- No prison can hold faith.

The gospel message of the Book of Acts is a bold statement of the Christian faith. Jesus is proclaimed Lord of all. Those of true faith are declared to be immune from fear. Even prison will not deter a true believer from living out his or her convictions.

The Least You Need to Know

- Peter was the leader of the Jerusalem church.
- The gospel was spread over the Roman Empire.
- The Sadducees formed strong opposition to the early Church.

- Stephen was martyred for his faith.
- Philip brought the gospel to the Samaritans.
- Peter and Paul focused on winning Gentiles.

18

The First New Age Movement (The Book of Revelation)

In This Chapter

- John, the author of Revelation
- Apocalyptic literature
- Rome = the Beast = Babylon
- The Church endures during great persecution
- The fall of Babylon
- Jesus, the Lamb, ushers in a new age

You will often hear it said that the Book of Revelation is complex and confusing. Many folks approach this book as if it is a book of magical incantations or formulas for strange potions. Others speak of it as a collection of dire predictions for the future—which is always thought to be coming any day now.

The truth is, the Book of Revelation is as black and white and clear-cut as any book in all of Hebrew or Christian Scripture. Once you understand a bit more about apocalyptic literature—which you soon will—the message of Revelation is as transparent as fine crystal.

Revelation is an old-fashioned story, or better put, series of stories. There are the good guys (the Church) and the bad guys (the Romans, especially emperors). There is an ongoing battle over turf (the Kingdom). There is the hero (the Lamb of God) who is, of course, Jesus. The hero lifts the good guys to victory, and the Kingdom finally begins to be built. The old days are gone, and the new days have begun. A very happy ending, only this time it is thought to be a beginning—the beginning of a New Age.

Will the Real John Please Stand Up?

The name John was common in Rome. It was also quite common within the church: John the Baptist, John the son of Zebedee, John the author of the Gospel, John the writer of the epistles, John the author of Revelation.

For decades scholars have sought to determine who were the authors of the various books in the Bible. The most obvious way to determine authorship has been to examine writing style and content. This means examining vocabulary, sentence structure, grammatical tendencies, and the spiritual as well as religious viewpoint. With all of this in mind, it appears that the Gospel of John and the first two epistles have the most in common.

Revelation is so stylistically different than John that it is widely held to be written by another John. We don't know who exactly, but here is what we do know about him:

- He possessed a deep faith.
- He spoke openly of his devotion to Jesus and remained faithful during times of horrid persecution.
- He was politically astute.

- He was a minister and wrote with genuine concern to the churches of Asia Minor.

- He knew the Torah inside and out.

- He was attracted to the apocalyptic writings in Hebrew Scripture, those that used dramatic images and stories.

- He was a Christian prophet.

- His writings were filled with warnings of impending disaster and the lure of evil.

- He was well known and well respected in Asia Minor.

- The Book of Revelation is accepted on the authority of his name alone.

Apocalyptic Literature

The Book of Revelation is sometimes referred to as the Apocalypse. *Apocalypse* in Greek means "to remove" and "to cover." The word *revelation* also has twin meanings: "to undo" and "to veil." An apocalypse, like a revelation, is a time when the veil will lift and the truth will be seen.

Think of it this way: You go to a play. The poor stage crew cannot get the curtain all the way up. You can see feet moving and hear voices, but you cannot make out the scene or the plot. Suddenly a rope gets unstuck and the curtain gratefully rises. Now you can see the play and make out what is happening on stage. More important, now you know the purpose of the story.

An apocalypse, or revelation, is like a stuck curtain rising on a play. Before all you could make out was a suggestion of the scene, a hint of the plot, a glimpse of the point of the play. Once the curtain rises—apocalypse/revelation—everything suddenly makes sense. You can see clearly. You understand.

Apocalyptic literature is a style of writing, like mystery or romance novels or a Stephen King book. Apocalyptic literature tends to have the following characteristics:

- It bears the name of an important religious person.

- It deals with present events in a very symbolic way.

- The writings often claim to have been written a long time ago and only recently recovered.

- There are many visions. The images grow more and more intense and more and more revealing. It is like a fog slowly lifting, revealing more and more of the future.

- There is an extensive use of symbols: animals, numbers, mysterious creatures, or wild weather.

- A crisis in history becomes the pivotal point of the story.

- The end is near.

- The reader is encouraged to remain faithful, even when times are dark and getting darker.

- Only God's intervention can help.

- It often refers to the writing of other prophets.

Apocalyptic literature is a creative editorializing of the news. This time the news is not about the rich and famous; it is not about morally bankrupt celebrities. This time the news is about the poor and the oppressed; it is a prediction.

God is coming, and those of the so-called good life (which is really the bad life) have numbered days. The last finally will be first; the first will be last. The world has been turned upside down. The Kingdom is up; the world is down.

Apocalyptic literature rips history in two. There is the old age that was filled with wickedness, greed, and corruption. There will be a new age that will be filled with peace, justice, and equality. There will be a single slicing event that will divide time in two. That event is the Apocalypse—the coming of Christ.

Rome

The Roman Empire had grown, reaching from Israel in the south, to England in the north. This expansion took more than 125 years and saw the rule of 11 different emperors. Roman rule was powerfully influenced by the personality of the emperor. Two emperors stand out for their emotional instability and propensity for evil and violence: Nero and Domitian.

Nero was vicious. He was the first significant persecutor of the Church, and the deaths of Peter and Paul are attributed to him. The great Roman fire was blamed on the Christians, and Nero, who may have caused the fire himself, had Christians tortured on a daily basis.

Domitian, who came to the throne some 13 years after Nero, took up where Nero left off. Domitian was known to cut off the heads of Christians and place them on large poles to mark the way to the Circus—where Christians were fed to wild animals.

Rome had also grown to be a nation of extraordinary wealth. It had not only expanded its territory but also its shipping and trade routes, developing a world-wide commerce of immense proportions. Rome was indeed the most powerful and richest nation on the planet.

Imagine what it must have felt like to be a Christian in these times:

- You had every reason to fear for your life.
- Nero and Domitian took emperor-worship seriously and did not take no for an answer.
- Persecution of Christians was rampant.
- Rome appeared to be blessed beyond measure by God.
- The Roman Empire claimed to be the real Kingdom.
- The Roman Emperor claimed to be the true king, the only soul with a chance of saving anyone.

Christians felt they were on shaky ground. The earth moved beneath their feet. They lived in terror. It was hard to maintain their faith. It was hard to see God as on their side. Where was their Messiah now?

Rome = the Beast

The Book of Revelation depicts Rome as a beast. This beast has the mouth of a lion, the feet of a bear, and the body of a leopard. Its seven heads represent seven emperors: Tiberius, Caligula, Claudius, Nero, Vespasian, Titus, and Domitian. Its 10 horns are these emperors plus three who only reigned for a brief time: Galba, Otha, and Vitellus.

For a significant period of time, Rome was viewed as a friend to Christianity. Paul often sought the help of the Roman government, acknowledging that he was often saved from the fury of the Jews by the Roman authorities. Paul went so far as to ask Christians to be obedient to those authorities. (Romans 13:1–6)

In Revelation, we get a completely altered portrait of Rome. Rome is now the ultimate enemy:

- Rome has become the champion of emperor-worship.
- Rome seeks to crush the Christian faith and anyone who does not swear allegiance to the emperor.
- Rome is the seat of Satan.
- Rome is the embodiment of the anti-Christ.
- Rome has no moral authority.
- Rome's wealth has left them spiritually and morally destitute.
- Rome is the bastion of death and decay.

In the Gospel of Luke, Jesus is tempted by the devil. One of three temptations is the offering of all the powers and riches of the world. Jesus is tempted by power and might, fame and fortune. But remember, it is the devil who makes the offer. It is the devil who is seen to control these worldly riches. For John, author of Revelation, Rome is home to the devil.

Rome = Babylon

It is hard for Americans to give the Book of Revelation an honest reading. The similarity between the nation of Rome and the United States is too obvious to ignore. It is tough for us to recognize when we sing or hear "The Hallelujah Chorus" that these words are sung by angels over the smoldering ruins of Rome—the greatest, wealthiest, and most powerful nation on earth.

Rome represented the opposite of the will and wishes of Jesus. It bore no resemblance to the Kingdom that Christ had instructed his followers to build. The Babylon of Revelation is a nation wicked to the core—Babylon is Rome.

Rome is the nation John describes as ...

- Having gained its wealth off the backs of the poor.
- Treating the needy with contempt.
- Avoiding service and sacrifice at all costs.
- Paying any price for pleasure—including its souls.
- Never having enough.
- Addicted to violence and death.
- Without humility or faith.
- A hard-hearted nation, void of mercy or compassion.

The fall of Babylon brought rejoicing in heaven. The fall of Rome was treated as an occasion of celebration. This nation, which did not care for its poor, sick, shattered, lonely, lost, or aged, deserved to lie in ruins.

The United States can learn a great deal from the Book of Revelation. So can the Church. Imagine the guts it would take to preach a prophetic message like the one found in Revelation!

Spread the Good Word

After all this I saw another angel come down from heaven with great authority, and the earth grew bright with his splendor. He gave a mighty shout, "Babylon is fallen—that great city is fallen! She has become the hideout of demons and evil spirits, a nest for filthy buzzards, and a den for dreadful beasts. For all the nations have drunk the wine of her passionate immorality. The rulers of the world have committed adultery with her, and merchants throughout the world have grown rich as a result of her luxurious living."

—Revelation 18:1–3

What Was Happening in the Church?

By A.D. 75, Asia Minor was no longer Paul's mission field. It had literally become the home of the Church. It was in Asia Minor that the Church really took root. Ephesus replaced Jerusalem as the spiritual center for the early Christians.

This new home posed very real spiritual threats:

- Christians were well known.
- If a Christian refused to worship the emperor, it would be hard to hide.
- Persecution was growing common—and acceptable.
- Christians were more integrated into mainstream culture.
- Christians were influenced by the materialistic world of Rome.
- Christianity had lost all of its founders and had no genuine leaders.
- Greed and power remained a powerful temptation.

John wrote Revelation as a means of offering focus and support to the Church. He attempted to offer Christians meaning for their suffering and hope for their future. His message was to tell Christians to endure these trials and tribulations: God is coming; we will emerge victorious; you will be rewarded for your faithfulness.

The Seven Visions

The bulk of the Book of Revelation consists of seven visions. These seven visions stage John's prophesy in eternity. In other words, John's message is for all people, everywhere, and for all time. The number seven was believed to be a perfect number, combining the four corners of the earth with the three-sided pyramid of the spiritual world. These seven visions are as follows:

- **The Seven Seals (6:1–8:1).** Jesus, the Lamb, breaks the seals and opens the seven scrolls.
- **The Seven Trumpets (8:2–11:15).** The intervention of God is heralded.

- **The Seven Visions of the Kingdom of the Beast (11:6–13:18).** The beast is the anti-Christ. The beast is the symbol for the Roman emperors.

- **The Seven Visions of the Coming of the Son of Man (14:1–20).** All followers of Jesus will bear his mark and be passed over at the time of the Apocalypse.

- **The Seven Bowls (15:1–16:21).** Rome will be judged for its wrongdoing.

- **The Seven Visions of the Fall of Babylon (17:1–19:10).** Rome will fall, to the delight of heaven.

- **The Seven Visions of the End (19:11–21:4).** God will create a new universe, where Christ and the saints will reign for 1,000 years.

The New Age

Throughout the Book of Revelation, we are told that the Lamb of God, Jesus Christ, will come again to reign victorious with the saints. The victory is not the winning of a battle; it is the claim of the ultimate triumph of good over evil.

The Book of Revelation describes this new age as the making of all things new; the transformation is total. The new age will produce a new Jerusalem, which is the kingdom of God; a new people, which is the communion of the saints; a new heaven; and a new earth. In this new age, a magnificent temple where God alone is worshipped will be built.

This new age is an eternal time and place where …

- Suffering, pain, and death do not exist.
- Honesty and truth reign.
- The saints will be rewarded.
- All needs, both physical and spiritual, are met.
- Christ reigns without threat.

The depiction of this new age is beautiful poetry. The imagery of precious stones and metals is abundant. I realize now that many of the images of heaven I had as a child, including pearly gates and streets of gold, were influenced by the Book of Revelation. The main theme of the new age is that it will be a time of peace and tranquility. It will be an era when the Grace of God is all that is known.

Spread the Good Word

Then I saw a new heaven and a new earth, for the old heaven and the old earth had disappeared. And the sea was also gone. And I saw the holy city, the new Jerusalem, coming down from God out of heaven like a beautiful bride prepared for her husband. I heard a loud shout from the throne, saying, "Look, the home of God is now among his people! He will live with them, and they will be his people. God himself will be with them. He will remove all their sorrows, and there will be no more death or sorrow or crying or pain. For the old world and its evils are gone forever."

—Revelation 21:1–4

Summary of the Main Points of Revelation

Here is a brief, simple, straightforward summation of the major points made by John in Revelation. I will try to be just as black and white here as John was in his composition of the Book of Revelation:

1. Evil exists; it is real.
2. A nation can be evil.
3. Evil is rooted in greed.
4. Evil is rooted in violence.

5. Evil is rooted in the lust for power.

6. Christians are called to be on the side of the poor, the needy, the outcast—the losers of the world.

7. The genuine good life is about service, sacrifice, and even suffering, all on behalf of God.

8. Christians must be merciful and forgiving in spite of persecution.

9. Jesus will reward his faithful followers.

10. Jesus will build his Kingdom.

Jesus ushers in a new age; heaven comes to earth; the Kingdom of justice and mercy is established; and the Christian saints reign victorious. A peace that passes all understanding covers the world—now it is finished!

The Least You Need to Know

- John the Prophet wrote the Book of Revelation during a time of horrific persecution of Christians by the Roman Empire.

- Rome is depicted by John as a sanctuary for Satan.

- The Church is challenged to remain faithful.

- Heaven will rejoice when Rome falls.

- Jesus, the Lamb, will usher in a new age of peace and tranquility.

- Christians will be rewarded for their perseverance and for remaining true to their calling to preach good news to the poor.